NOW
WE'RE
TALKING!

21 Days to High-Performance
Instructional Leadership

JUSTIN BAEDER

Solution Tree | Press

a division of
Solution Tree

555 North Morton Street
Bloomington, IN 47404
800.733.6786 (toll free) / 812.336.7700
FAX: 812.336.7790

email: info@SolutionTree.com
SolutionTree.com

Printed in the United States of America

Library of Congress Cataloging-in-Publication Data

Names: Baeder, Justin, author.
Title: Now we're talking! : 21 days to high-performance instructional
   leadership / Justin Baeder.
Description: Bloomington, IN : Solution Tree Press, [2017] | Includes
   bibliographical references and index.
Identifiers: LCCN 2017020033 | ISBN 9781936764204 (perfect bound)
Subjects: LCSH: Observation (Educational method) | Educational leadership. |
   Teacher-administrator relationships. | School improvement programs.
Classification: LCC LB1731.6 .B34 2017 | DDC 370.71/1--dc23 LC record available at
   https://lccn.loc.gov/2017020033

Solution Tree
Jeffrey C. Jones, CEO
Edmund M. Ackerman, President

Solution Tree Press
President and Publisher: Douglas M. Rife
Editorial Director: Sarah Payne-Mills
Art Director: Rian Anderson
Managing Production Editor: Caroline Cascio
Production Editor: Alissa Voss
Senior Editor: Amy Rubenstein
Copy Editor: Miranda Addonizio
Proofreader: Elisabeth Abrams
Text and Cover Designer: Laura Cox
Editorial Assistants: Jessi Finn and Kendra Slayton

Acknowledgments

This book would not have been possible without the dedicated mentorship of the instructional leaders who guided me through my career with Seattle Public Schools—BiHoa Caldwell, Ron Howard, Jewell Woods, Dan Warren, Pat Sander, Scott Whitbeck, and Phil Brockman—as well as the more than ten thousand leaders around the world who have taken up the challenge to make daily classroom visits a core part of their practice.

—Justin Baeder

Solution Tree Press would like to thank the following reviewers:

Matthew Blackmore
Principal
Carlisle High School
Carlisle, Iowa

Cara Kimball
Principal
Lincoln Elementary School
Hastings, Nebraska

Susan Myers
Principal
Walter S. Mills-Parole
    Elementary School
Annapolis, Maryland

Rachel Jones
Principal
Gurney Elementary School
Chagrin Falls, Ohio

Louis Lim
Vice Principal
Bayview Secondary School
Richmond Hill, Ontario Canada

Richard J. Noblett
Director of Student Achievement
Baldwin Park Unified
    School District
Baldwin Park, California

Bill Powers
Principal
Cherokee Middle School
Springfield, Missouri

Kristin Smetana
Principal
Riverside Brookfield
  High School
Riverside, Illinois

Table of Contents

Week 3: High-Impact Instructional Conversations . . . 95

Week 4: High-Performance Instructional Leadership Enhancement **137**

About the Author

 **Justin Baeder** is director of The Principal Center, where he helps school and district administrators build capacity for instructional leadership. Prior to starting The Principal Center, Baeder served as a teacher, head teacher, and principal in Seattle Public Schools, finishing his ten-year career in Seattle as principal of Olympic View Elementary. His professional interests focus on strategic planning, goal setting, organizational learning, and productivity. Driven by the belief that leaders belong in classrooms—where the most important work is being done—he created the 21-Day Instructional Leadership Challenge (www.instructional leadershipchallenge.com), which has helped more than ten thousand leaders from fifty countries develop the habit of getting into classrooms and having evidence-based conversations with teachers.

He has contributed to *School Administrator*, *Principal News Magazine*, *Principal Magazine*, *Principal Navigator Magazine*, and *Education Week*. Baeder presents regularly at state and national conferences, including the Association for Supervision and Curriculum Development, Learning Forward, and the National Association of Elementary School Principals, and he has been an invited keynote speaker at numerous state principals' conferences in California, Pennsylvania, Washington, Texas, Arkansas, Utah, North Dakota, West Virginia, and Wyoming.

Baeder is currently a doctoral candidate studying principal productivity at the University of Washington, and is a graduate of the Danforth Educational Leadership Program at the University of Washington. He holds a master's degree in education with a focus on curriculum and instruction from Seattle University, and a bachelor's degree in science education from Harding University.

To learn more about Baeder's work, visit The Principal Center (www .principalcenter.com) or follow @eduleadership on Twitter.

To book Justin Baeder for professional development, contact pd@ SolutionTree.com.

Introduction

S hould school administrators visit classrooms? If you ask any education leader, you'll undoubtedly hear enthusiastic support for the idea. As leaders, we understand intuitively that instructional leaders belong in classrooms because effective classroom visits can lead to significant improvements in teaching and learning.

Yet we know the reality is far from our ideal: it's hard to get into classrooms on a regular basis, so the practice is far less common than we'd like. Since much of my professional work focuses on helping administrators spend more time in classrooms, I've made a habit of asking teachers how often they receive helpful feedback from an administrator. The answer is almost always the same: somewhere between *once a year* and *never*. When I ask administrators how much feedback they received as classroom teachers, they too report receiving either once-yearly feedback or none at all.

These reports from the field match data from a study by Jason A. Grissom, Susanna Loeb, and Benjamin Master (2013), who found that while principals in their study spent 12.7 percent of their time on instructional leadership activities, including 5.4 percent of the workday on classroom walkthroughs, they devoted only 0.5 percent of their time to coaching teachers. Across the span of a school year, this equates to less than ten hours—not per teacher, but total. In the same study,

Grissom et al. (2013) found that informal classroom walkthroughs were the most common instructional leadership activity principals engaged in, but these walkthroughs had a negative correlation with student achievement gains, which the authors suggest is "because principals often do not use walkthroughs as part of a broader school improvement strategy" (p. 433), but rather as a means of collecting data.

Why are we failing to tap into the potential of regular classroom visits? Having tried a variety of approaches to classroom walkthroughs as a principal, I believe it's because we don't find our visits to classrooms to be professionally rewarding—for ourselves as leaders, or for our teachers. We may strive to provide high-quality feedback, but find that it never seems to have the impact on instruction that we hope. Deep down, we know we need to be in classrooms, but we also have doubts about whether our standard approaches to providing feedback are effective enough to justify the time and effort involved. Since there is no shortage of other work to keep leaders busy outside the classroom, it's no wonder we don't make much time for classroom visits.

In this book, you'll discover an approach to instructional leadership that recognizes the importance of getting into classrooms on a daily basis, but without the drawbacks of traditional walkthrough models. I call this approach *high-performance instructional leadership*. The core practice is simple: visit three classrooms a day for five to ten minutes each, and after observing, have a brief conversation with the teacher to make sense of what you've seen and to learn more about the teacher's thinking and instructional decision making. This basic practice holds surprising power to build capacity for instructional leadership in your school.

The Importance of Effective Instructional Leadership

What is *instructional leadership*? It's not just a matter of providing feedback to teachers or planning professional development; it's about doing what you need to do to run and improve the school as a learning organization. I define *instructional leadership* as *the practice of making and implementing operational and improvement decisions*. Building capacity for instructional leadership, then, is a matter of helping everyone in the organization—teachers and administrators alike—obtain better information for better decision making.

Unlike other approaches, the high-performance instructional leadership model doesn't emphasize supervision, coaching, or data collection—though it facilitates all three. Instead, the purpose of visiting classrooms is to simply *pay attention*—to learn what teachers are doing—so you can have evidence-based conversations about practice. This is a subtle but key difference, driven by the reality that as an instructional leader, you play a critical decision-making role in your school. Henry Mintzberg (1973), in his classic text *The Nature of Managerial Work*, explains that *decisional* roles are unique to leadership positions:

> Probably the most crucial part of the manager's work—the part that justifies his great authority and his powerful access to information—is that performed in his decisional roles. These roles involve the manager in the strategy-making process in his organization. Strategy-making can be defined simply as the process by which significant organizational decisions are made and interrelated. (p. 77)

School administrators need rich, firsthand information about teaching and learning in order to make good operational and instructional decisions, and the best place to gain that information—the best setting for continued professional learning—is the classroom.

It's my goal to help you develop the habit of visiting classrooms and having evidence-rich, framework-linked conversations with teachers, every single day, so you can increase your effectiveness as an instructional leader. The model you'll discover in this book will help you avoid the awkwardness and conflict that often accompany traditional walkthroughs and teacher observations, and instead reap the professional rewards of stronger relationships with teachers and better information about the teaching and learning taking place in your school.

While I wrote this book with school-based administrators in mind, you will also find its perspective valuable if you're an instructional coach, school improvement facilitator, or central office leader. You may not be able to adopt this exact approach to visiting classrooms and having conversations with teachers, but the high-performance instructional leadership model reflects a philosophy of professional learning that applies to instructional leaders of all types, not just administrators.

This book grew out of a global online experiment called the 21-Day Instructional Leadership Challenge (visit www.instructionalleadership challenge.com for more information). I set out to help school leaders get into classrooms more frequently and have a greater impact on instruction, and with over ten thousand participants in more than fifty countries, it's safe to say the experiment has been a success. Every day, instructional leaders are choosing to spend their time where the real work of schools takes place: in the classroom. Over the course of a single school year, many leaders are now making five hundred or more classroom visits. Visit www.instructionalleadershipchallenge.com/500 to see their comments and photos.

Leaders who know what that work looks like, day in and day out, are more effective decision makers and have a greater impact on classroom practice. It's my goal that you'll join the global cadre of instructional leaders who strive to visit classrooms daily—not just occasionally, but consistently.

About This Book

I have organized this book into twenty-one chapters and designed it for you to read and implement over a period of twenty-one school days. Each chapter concludes with an action to complete that day, so if you prefer to read ahead, or if you're reading the book when school is not in session, simply go back and complete the action items, in order, whenever school is in session. Some of these action items relate to your visits to classrooms, and others will help you develop systems to manage your workload and make time to get out of the office and into classrooms. Over the course of twenty-one days, you'll visit each teacher you supervise at least once—what we refer to as a *cycle* of visits—and we'll also discuss what to do in future visits, so you can lay the right foundation.

The first part (chapters 1 through 5), which you may read over five school days, will address high-performance instructional leadership fundamentals. It will discuss why instructional leaders belong in classrooms, introduce the high-performance instructional leadership model, and compare this model to several other classroom walkthrough models with which you may already be familiar. You will also plan and complete your first day of classroom visits.

This introductory section also describes the first three cycles of visits, which will gradually increase in intensity as you develop your skills in high-performance instructional leadership. Although you will not participate in the third and most complex stage of visits at this point, I describe the third cycle (in chapter 5, page 43) so you have a complete picture of the model and an eye to what you will work toward as you improve your instructional leadership skills. You may revisit these fundamental aspects at any time throughout the twenty-one-day process.

The second part (chapters 6 through 10) delves into high-performance habits. Many of these administrative habits, such as making time to visit classrooms, keeping interruptions under control, and organizing your to-do lists, will assist you in your efforts to get into classrooms *daily*.

The third part (chapters 11 through 15) emphasizes the crux of the high-performance instructional leadership model—learning how to have high-impact instructional conversations with teachers. These chapters discuss going beyond data collection and learning the skills required to have productive, evidence-based conversations with teachers.

The fourth part (chapters 16 through 21) builds on the results of your classroom visits. It discusses improving your feedback repertoire, balancing formal with informal evaluation responsibilities, identifying improvements to make, and scaling high-impact instructional visits across your school and district.

I've arranged the chapters and action items in a sequence that will help you adopt a *bias toward action*, because—while it will take the entire book to fully share this instructional leadership model and its many benefits—I don't want you to postpone taking action. Take small steps daily to implement the systems and strategies I describe in the following chapters, and in about a month's time, you'll develop powerful new instructional leadership habits that will increase your impact on student learning, reduce your stress level, and strengthen your professional relationships.

WEEK I

High-Performance Instructional Leadership Fundamentals

In this part, we explore the fundamentals of the high-performance instructional leadership model. You'll learn why and how to make a habit of classroom visits that are frequent, brief, substantive, open ended, evidence based, criterion referenced, and conversation oriented. We look at each of these features in detail and contrast the model with other supervision and instructional leadership approaches so you can get started right away with integrating the high-performance instructional leadership model into your existing practices.

Understanding Why Instructional Leaders Belong in Classrooms

"*Genchi genbutsu*—Go to the real place." This Japanese phrase suggests that wise leaders should spend significant time in the spaces where the core work of their organization takes place, because that's where the challenges and opportunities become clear. If school administrators are to be leaders of learning, we must get into classrooms on a daily basis. Yet this imperative to "go to the real place" is taken most seriously not in schools, but in Toyota factories, where it is a key principle (Liker, 2004). The Toyota manufacturing system expects managers and supervisors to regularly visit the shop floors where the workers are doing their jobs instead of managing them from the comfort of their offices. Without talking with their front-line employees, solving problems together, and gaining perspective on what the work truly entails, leaders simply cannot lead. If this is true for leaders in highly routinized environments like Toyota factories, it's even more crucial in dynamic, human-centric organizations like schools, where decisions are more complex and relationships are key. If we aspire to be high-performance instructional leaders, I believe we must spend substantial time in classrooms, where the core work of teaching and learning takes place. For only through classroom visits, as you will learn in this chapter, can we gain decisional information, build strong professional relationships, and enhance professional development.

Gain Decisional Information

Let's return for a moment to our definition of instructional leadership: *the practice of making and implementing operational and improvement decisions.* One of the most valuable benefits of spending time in classrooms is what Mintzberg (1973) terms *decisional information*—information that directly informs the decisions leaders must make. For principals and other administrators who must make high-stakes decisions on behalf of their organizations, information about what's actually taking place in classrooms is a priceless asset. Which teachers are ready to take on new professional challenges, and which are at risk for nonrenewal? Among students, who is struggling, who is thriving, and why? What impact is professional development having on teaching practice? Did we choose the right curriculum? How can we best deploy our coaching resources for maximum impact? As effective managers, we must seek the answers to these questions—and they're answers that we can only find in classrooms.

For principals and other administrators who must make high-stakes decisions on behalf of their organizations, information about what's actually taking place in classrooms is a priceless asset.

In my work with school and district leaders, I've rarely encountered anyone who wants to be known as a manager rather than a leader, perhaps because the term *management* has taken on a stigma through its association with maintaining the status quo. Certainly, there are many aspects of the status quo that should make us uncomfortable and that should prompt us to pursue change. Yet the status quo also produces all of the good results we're currently getting—a fact we often overlook in our earnest efforts to lead change. For this reason, effective management is at the heart of my definition of instructional leadership—the practice of making and implementing operational and improvement decisions. It's important to understand your school's current practices—good and bad—in order to make sound decisions about what to sustain by managing well, and what to change. For example, a principal who wants to introduce new literacy strategies will have a hard time persuading and helping teachers to adopt new practices without an understanding of their current practices in literacy instruction. Abraham Zaleznik (2004) frames management as problem-solving work, and solving problems requires current, firsthand information about the problems. Effective instructional leaders need decisional information, and that means we need to be in classrooms.

Build Strong Professional Relationships

To lead the changes our students need us to make on their behalf, we must form strong professional relationships with the teachers we instruct, because it's only through relationships that we can inspire the necessary level of commitment to produce change (Bryk & Schneider, 2002). There's no better way to strengthen professional relationships than to have substantive instructional conversations on a regular basis, as Charlotte Danielson (2015), author of the most widely used teacher evaluation framework, notes in her book *Talk About Teaching! Leading Professional Conversations*. Danielson (2015) writes that "informal conversations are critical to the culture in a school; they help convey respect and build trust across the hierarchy" (p. 20), and argues that when "conducted in an environment of trust and respect, they offer important opportunities for professional learning" (p. 25).

Yet if these conversations are to be more than mere philosophizing, they must stem from firsthand experience with teaching and learning—experience that teachers and leaders gain together in the classroom, where the core work of teaching and learning takes place. If spending time in classrooms is essential for effective management, it's even more essential for high-performance instructional leadership and for building strong professional relationships.

Enhance Professional Development

When you visit classrooms, you can see for yourself what teachers and students are doing on a daily basis. This information is valuable in its own right, but it becomes dramatically more valuable when put into context through a conversation with the teacher. These conversations can provide some of the best professional development available anywhere, for both the instructional leader and the teacher (Danielson, 2015). Discussing evidence from the lesson, relating it to shared expectations, and talking about next steps is an incredibly powerful process.

Discussing evidence from the lesson, relating it to shared expectations, and talking about next steps is an incredibly powerful process.

It gives the teacher information about his or her own practice, and it gives you information about both what teachers are doing and how they're thinking about their work.

For instructional leaders who are also organizational leaders, the value of this information is even greater. Consider the huge range of decisions school administrators must make or advise on: strategic planning, scheduling, professional development, teacher evaluation, and so on. The list is nearly endless. Every one of these decisions—and your overall leadership—will be better if you are equipped with current, thorough knowledge of what teachers are doing and how they think about teaching and learning.

Day 1 Action Challenge: Determine Your Baseline for Classroom Visits

If high-performance instructional leadership is to fulfill its potential, you can't limit it to special occasions, specific projects, or year-end teacher evaluations. Every school leader visits classrooms from time to time, but occasional visits aren't enough. You need both a clear model to follow and a disciplined habit to put classroom visits into practice consistently.

The first step is to take an honest look at your current practice. Review your records, such as walkthrough logs or your calendar, and determine how much time you typically spend in classrooms. The following questions may help you in your assessment.

- How many times per year do you visit each teacher on an informal basis?
- On average, how much time elapses between two visits to a given teacher's classroom?
- How many total classroom visits do you make in a year?
- On how many days per month do you visit no classrooms at all (such as days you're at district meetings)?

▸ How many teachers have gone a month or more without seeing you in their classroom?

If you don't have access to clear records, it's perfectly fine to estimate, but be honest with yourself and answer as many of these questions as possible. Because we tend to overestimate our time in classrooms and underestimate our tendency to avoid certain teachers, I've worded the questions in several different ways to help you determine your baseline accurately. We tend to recall our best days and extrapolate them to the rest of the year, so if you visited five classrooms one day in October, good for you—but is this typical behavior comparable to other days of the year? Ensure that you are honest in your responses.

Acknowledging your current practice is the first step. Don't exaggerate, but don't berate yourself, either. If your baseline is zero, you've no doubt been doing other important work to lead your school. And you've come to the right place to help you improve your instructional leadership.

2

Following the High-Performance Instructional Leadership Model

What can you do to maximize your impact on teacher practice when you visit classrooms? Most instructional leaders conduct mandatory formal observations and make an effort to visit classrooms more often, but these visits often seem limited in value—especially prearranged formal observations, which Marshall (2013) describes, in his experience as a principal, as "dog-and-pony shows—contrived, unrepresentative, nervous-making lessons solely for my benefit" (p. 60). Given all the other pressures we face, if classroom visits don't provide considerable benefits for both instructional leaders and teachers, there is simply no incentive to make time for visits on a consistent basis.

To ensure that our time in classrooms has a positive impact on student learning and is professionally rewarding for everyone involved, the high-performance instructional leadership model consists of classroom visits that are:

- **Frequent**—Approximately eighteen biweekly visits per teacher per year
- **Brief**—Around five to fifteen minutes
- **Substantive**—More than just making an appearance

- **Open ended**—Focused on the teacher's instructional decision making, not just narrow data collection
- **Evidence based**—Centered on what actually happens in the classroom
- **Criterion referenced**—Linked to a shared set of standards or expectations
- **Conversation oriented**—Designed to lead to rich, engaging conversations between teachers and instructional leaders

I drew these characteristics from existing models and practices in our profession (see chapter 3 for detailed comparisons), but here they form a unique approach designed to give teachers and instructional leaders the greatest possible benefits from classroom visits. In this chapter, we explore each of these criteria in a bit more depth. I will also discuss the concept of a *shared instructional framework*—expectations shared between teachers and instructional leaders that collectively define professional practice and performance for teachers at a school—and encourage leaders to identify their own instructional frameworks.

Make Frequent Visits

If we want to see meaningful results from our time in classrooms, it's only logical that we commit to an adequate dose for our efforts. Kim Marshall (2013) notes that administrators are not present for 99.9 percent of the instruction that takes place in classrooms, yet are responsible for obtaining enough information to evaluate teachers fairly. In sampling terms, visiting a classroom only once or twice per year gives an administrator a very limited perspective on a teacher's practice. Grissom et al. (2013) found that time spent coaching teachers is associated with higher student achievement in mathematics. Yet, they also found that, on average, only 0.5 percent of principals' time was devoted to coaching teachers, which can be expected to produce student learning gains of less than 0.05 percent of a standard deviation—far too small a difference to notice. We must visit teachers frequently if we want to have a noticeable impact on their practice.

We must visit teachers frequently if we want to have a noticeable impact on their practice.

How often is often enough? It depends on the nature of your role and the number of teachers you supervise. A two-week rotation—visiting every teacher you supervise every other week—strikes a balance between frequency and practicality for most school-based administrators who are responsible for evaluating teachers. If you visit 10 percent of your teachers daily in a 180-day school year, you'll reach everyone approximately eighteen times, not including formal observations or other types of visits to classrooms. Depending on how many teachers you supervise, this will typically require two to four visits per day. If you're part of an administrative team that shares evaluation responsibilities, plan to visit only the teachers you supervise.

However, if you supervise an especially large number of teachers, or if you're not in a school-based administrative role, it may not be feasible to establish a two-week rotation. Instead, focus on a daily target of three visits, or a weekly target of fifteen visits. On the other hand, if you're a coach providing intensive support to a group of five new teachers, your visit frequency will be higher. For the sake of simplicity, we'll treat three visits per day as a standard target throughout this book.

Make Brief Visits

In order to form a sustainable habit, it's essential to keep your classroom visits brief. Frequent visits become virtually impossible to sustain if they swell to thirty minutes or more. As the length of a visit increases, the chance of scheduling conflicts and interruptions multiplies dramatically. Additionally, school schedules often break down into five- or even one-minute increments, creating awkward blocks of time. Fitting half-hour or longer visits into a schedule full of passing periods, recesses, and lunch periods is a formidable challenge. The odds you'd be able to stay in a classroom for most of a lesson without interruption, three times a day, every day, are slim indeed.

The solution is to keep your visits brief enough to be practical, but long enough to be meaningful. A one- to three-minute visit may be long enough to make an appearance, but it's not long enough to provide you with the information you'll need to have a substantive conversation with the teacher. For most visits, five to fifteen minutes tends to be the sweet spot, with rapidly diminishing returns beyond the fifteen-minute mark. Marshall (2013) notes that "After five or ten minutes, the amount of new information levels off and then gradually declines for the remainder of the period" (p. 66). I have sometimes found it worthwhile to stay a bit longer to see the conclusion of an activity, but it usually takes less than ten minutes to see enough to fuel a substantive conversation. If you arrive during a time that won't lead to a useful conversation—say, because students are taking a test—you can stay a bit longer or come back later, but as a rule of thumb, ten minutes is a reasonable goal to strive for.

Make Substantive Visits

For a classroom visit to make a difference in your leadership and in the teacher's practice, it must focus on significant issues of teaching and learning. However, you will need to develop relationships with teachers before this will be possible. You'll want to initiate your first cycle of visits in a nonthreatening manner that builds trust, and this may mean that conversations in your first cycle are less substantive than you'd like. After your initial round of visits to classrooms, though, you'll be able to delve deeper in these conversations so you can gain insight into teachers' decision making and strengthen your understanding of teacher and student needs.

One caution is in order: the imperative to make our visits substantive doesn't mean we always need to provide suggestions for improvement. In fact, making suggestions to teachers following brief visits is often counterproductive (Danielson, 2015). Rather than striving to "fix" teachers' lessons by pointing out minor opportunities for improvement, our focus should be on discussing—verbally and in writing—the dynamics at work in the classroom, with reference to a shared set of expectations, such as a curriculum guide or teacher evaluation rubric. Through this dialogue, we stand a much better chance of having a positive impact on students.

Make Open-Ended Visits

These visits to classrooms should result in learning for both the teacher and the instructional leader, but I didn't design them to produce a rating of the teacher or the lesson. While every educator has a personal understanding of what a good lesson should look like, the reality is that a single visit doesn't provide enough information for a sound evaluation of the lesson's overall effectiveness. As the instructional leader and teacher talk about what happened in the lesson—in a brief conversation or perhaps via email later—the focus should be on whether the lesson was effective in achieving the teacher's aims, which may be more complex than a visitor can ascertain during one visit. This requires that the instructional leader observe with an open mind and treat the teacher as the expert (Danielson, 2015).

Too often, supervisors march into classrooms, clipboards in hand, and rate elements such as lesson design, instructional strategies, student grouping, student engagement, and countless other aspects of teaching without attending to the essential question of whether the lesson accomplishes what the *teacher* intends. This leads to frustration and resistance from teachers who may be genuinely interested in feedback—if they have a say in what they'd like feedback on. If we enter each classroom with an open mind, we can focus on addressing the issues that are most relevant to the teacher. For example, if a lesson is effective at helping students achieve the selected learning targets, but those targets aren't rigorous enough, prescribing a different instructional technique won't help because increasing rigor is a planning issue. When we seek to understand the teacher's approach and consider it on its own merits, we can have more substantive, impactful conversations that change teacher practice in meaningful ways and result in higher levels of learning for students.

Make Evidence-Based Visits

The goal of classroom visits in the high-performance instructional leadership model is to obtain firsthand information from the classroom—where the work of teaching and learning is taking place—to inform subsequent conversations and decisions. When an instructional leader gives only a vague description of what happened in the lesson, such as "Students were not paying attention while you gave instructions," it's difficult to map the relationships between teacher actions and students' experience. Richly descriptive evidence, on the other hand, can lead to deeper explorations of the impact instruction is having on student learning.

The goal of classroom visits in the high-performance instructional leadership model is to obtain firsthand information from the classroom—where the work of teaching and learning is taking place—to inform subsequent conversations and decisions.

Taking descriptive, low-inference notes can both help you recall what happened and give the teacher—who was too busy teaching to take his or her own notes—a record of what transpired. For example, if you noted that one group of students was talking, and the teacher immediately went and worked with that group to get them started, this low-inference evidence can lead to a richer discussion than a more judgmental comment such as "Students were not paying attention." Equipped with this written record, both parties can remain open to new interpretations of the lesson based on their conversation.

Because the word *evidence* may have negative connotations for teachers, you may wish to simply refer to your written records as *notes*.

Make Criterion-Referenced Visits

Descriptive evidence doesn't stand on its own; it only gains meaning within a set of shared expectations. These shared expectations are drawn from teacher evaluation rubrics, professional standards, curriculum, professional development, strategic plans, and other resources that collectively define professional practice and performance for teachers at your school. We'll refer to these expectations collectively as the *instructional framework* that teachers and instructional leaders share.

Even an evidence-based conversation can devolve into little more than philosophizing if it's not anchored in a shared instructional framework. When the instructional framework takes on the role of defining effective practice, the instructional leader can step out of the role of judge and into a more collegial role. When the framework becomes like a third participant in the conversation between teacher and instructional leader, the discussion can become less focused on evaluation and more focused on evidence-based insights.

It's important to distinguish between a shared instructional framework and an observation checklist or rating tool. Some instructional frameworks' criteria describe practice writ large, not individual lessons or activities within a lesson. Not everything that characterizes effective practice will be visible in a single lesson, so we must resist the tendency to turn overall *evaluation* criteria into *observation* criteria. Additionally, many sources of shared expectations, such as curriculum guides, are not designed to evaluate teachers, but rather to aid teacher decision-making. Rather than using the language of your instructional framework to rate teachers during your visits, you'll find it most helpful to use this language as the vocabulary of professional conversation.

Make Conversation-Oriented Visits

The immediate goal of spending time in classrooms is to inform the follow-up conversation that must then take place, either face to face or via email. In this conversation, you can provide firsthand observations that can eliminate the teacher's blind spots and provide rich fodder for discussion. It's critical, though, that this discussion occur as a conversation and not as a cross-examination. The goal is not to point out flaws and make suggestions for improvement; it's to enhance both participants' understanding of the teacher's current practice as well as the ideal of the instructional framework. This understanding can, in turn, lead to better decisions by both the instructional leader and the teacher.

It's not unusual for even the most experienced instructional leaders to walk away from these conversations having learned a great deal and having made few or no suggestions. The teacher learns and improves his or her practice not by accepting suggestions, but by developing a deeper understanding of professional practice through evidence-rich, criterion-referenced conversation.

The high-performance instructional leadership model—centered on classroom visits that are frequent, brief, substantive, open ended, evidence based, criterion referenced, and conversation oriented—leads to stronger collegial relationships, better decision making by both parties, and a culture of continual learning.

Day 2 Action Challenge: Find Your Framework

Make a list of documents that comprise your overall instructional framework. The following questions may help you as you compile your list.

- What formal document contains your teacher evaluation criteria?
- Where can you find descriptions of curriculum-specific instructional practices that teachers have been trained to use?
- What professional development experiences and materials have shaped your school's collective definition of effective practice?

Compile a list of these sources, and as soon as possible, gather the actual documents. This will aid you in having framework-linked conversations about classroom practice in the coming weeks. I will elaborate on developing a shared instructional framework with teachers in chapter 13 (page 115).

3

Acknowledging Related Instructional Leadership, Supervision, and Walkthrough Models

In your school, you likely exercise instructional leadership in the context of a multitude of district, state, and professional expectations and policies, which may make it difficult to develop a well-aligned, coherent approach. In this chapter, we explore how the high-performance instructional leadership model compares to other models for instructional supervision and leadership that you may have previously experienced—and may currently be using. Specifically, I compare the high-performance instructional leadership model to formal teacher observations, annual formal evaluations, learning walks and instructional rounds, instructional coaching, and hybrid models of instructional supervision. The reality is that in most schools, several of these models operate at once, perhaps without anyone ever explicitly comparing them. By the end of this chapter, you'll be clear on how you can achieve your instructional leadership goals in classrooms, without pursuing conflicting aims.

Formal Teacher Observations

The most familiar instructional supervision model is the formal teacher observation process, which most public schools and many private schools require.

While the details vary, typically:

▸ Formal observations are required by law or policy, and contribute to the final evaluation, which has some bearing on the teacher's employment status (Danielson, 2015)

▸ Classroom observations are preannounced—in other words, the teacher knows when the administrator is coming (Marshall, 2013)

▸ Pre- or postconferences, or both, in which the teacher and administrator discuss the lesson, are required

▸ The administrator stays for the entire lesson, or at least a substantial portion of it, and may take copious notes

▸ The administrator may provide a written report, which becomes part of the teacher's employment file, and the need to produce this report dictates many aspects of the interaction between administrator and teacher (Danielson, 2015)

▸ One or more formal observations serve as a key element of the final annual evaluation (though not all teachers may be required to have a formal observation every year)

These features may be obvious, but they will serve as important points of contrast as we explore other models in this chapter.

In many schools, individual teachers and administrators do not have the discretion to modify or opt out of the formal observation and evaluation process, which may be governed by board policies, collective bargaining agreements, and even state law. For this reason, if you are responsible for evaluating teachers, you'll want to conduct your high-performance instructional leadership visits *in addition to*, rather than instead of, formal observations.

Assuming you're required to conduct formal observations, how can the high-performance instructional leadership model fit into your overall instructional leadership plan? Perhaps the greatest benefit is *context*: because these visits are unannounced and much more frequent, they provide a far better indication of teachers' typical practice than formal observations, which both teachers and administrators understand are often *dog-and-pony shows* that vary markedly from typical practice (Marshall, 2013). Depending on your teacher contract, you may or may not be able to use written evidence from unannounced visits in the formal evaluation process. However, you can have a much better sense of each teacher's areas of strength and weakness if you've made a habit of visiting classrooms daily, and you can differentiate your approach to collecting evidence as needed.

Annual Formal Evaluations

Most teachers receive a formal year-end evaluation, but in too many schools, administrators base their evaluations on little—or even no—direct observation of classroom practice. It's no wonder that so many educators regard the evaluation process as a waste of time (Danielson, 2015). Even so, it has the potential to be an essential part of our quality assurance efforts as instructional leaders. We owe our students the guarantee that all teachers are meeting certain standards, and we owe our teachers a fair shake in that process; we can fulfill both of these obligations only if we have firsthand evidence of teacher practice. You may find that your notes from informal classroom visits are among your best sources of evidence and insight as you prepare final evaluations for each teacher.

Regardless of whether formal observations are required, instructional leaders *belong* in classrooms. Only with the sense of context you gain from regular classroom visits can you collect the right evidence and draw valid conclusions about teacher performance. Many aspects of teaching aren't directly observable during formal observations—practices such as planning, collaborating, reviewing assessment results, and contacting families—yet are critical to the final evaluation. Some of the best evidence and insight into these non-observable aspects of teaching will come from the conversations you have with teachers after visiting their classrooms.

Only with the sense of context you gain from regular classroom visits can you collect the right evidence and draw valid conclusions about teacher performance.

Mini-Observations

Kim Marshall (2013), in his book *Rethinking Teacher Supervision and Evaluation*, argues that the formal *dog-and-pony show* observation process is deeply flawed, and that with modest changes, instructional leaders can modify it into a highly effective system of mini-observations. In Marshall's (2013) approach, mini-observations are:

‣ Unannounced, so there's no preconference

‣ Brief—in the fifteen-minute range

‣ Followed by a face-to-face postconference—either on the spot, later in the day, or the next day

‣ Accompanied by a written report similar to, but briefer than, a formal observation report

‣ Frequent, with every teacher receiving approximately ten mini-observations each year

Because formal observations are time consuming, Marshall (2013) advocates wholly replacing the typical system of prearranged formal observations with unannounced, shorter observations. If you're able to secure approval to switch from preannounced formal observations to unscheduled mini-observations, you will likely find that Marshall's (2013) approach provides much richer evidence and much more thorough documentation of teacher practice, which can result in much more substantive annual evaluations. However, you may find that this system is difficult to sustain due to the time commitment required to conduct, discuss, and write about ten observations for each teacher, which will take at least thirty to sixty minutes each.

Data-Collection Walkthroughs

What about walkthrough models that bear more similarity to the high-performance instructional leadership model I describe in this book? There are many approaches to brief classroom visits, but perhaps the most common—and the most problematic—is the data-collection walkthrough. Though the professional literature supporting data-collection walkthroughs is sparse (Kachur, Stout, & Edwards, 2010), I have found this model to be widespread and persistent—perhaps because central office leaders, such as superintendents, often mandate it. In data- collection walkthroughs, an administrator visits classrooms to collect evidence about specific practices or learning conditions—for example, to determine whether teachers are using a questioning strategy the district is promoting, or to collect data to determine what percentage of students is actively engaged. These *look-fors* may focus instructional leaders' attention on certain issues, but at the expense of making the process less beneficial overall.

Data-collection walkthroughs are problematic for several reasons. First, the focus of the data collection may not be relevant to the current activities taking place in the classroom; this wastes significant time. Second, it typically has no value for the teachers being observed, who have no choice in what they want feedback on and instead receive feedback on look-fors that may have little relevance to the lesson. Third, while the school or district may put the data to good use, they're of limited value to the instructional leader, who lacks the discretion to focus on the most relevant issues that emerge in the moment, or the school's current instructional priorities, when collecting mandated forms of data.

Are data-collection walkthroughs even effective ways to obtain reliable data about classroom practice? On a practical level, administrators are among the highest-paid educators in most school systems and have many other pressing priorities that interfere with their ability to adhere to a data-collection protocol. From a scientific perspective, it's worth asking whether educators can draw any reliable conclusions from the data that walkthroughs generate. Schools too often sweep questions about sampling under the rug: How many unannounced walkthroughs are necessary for generating trustworthy data about an individual teacher's practice? How should we distribute walkthroughs throughout the school day? How consistent is the observer from one walkthrough to the next, and what degree of inter-rater reliability has been established? Without solid answers to these questions, districts should treat walkthrough data as anecdotal rather than scientific.

Data-collection walkthroughs can also have unintended consequences that undermine their viability; for example, if teachers know that administrators expect to see a certain strategy when they visit, they will quickly learn to use that strategy any time administrators are in the room. During my tenure as a principal, we taught teachers to use a strategy known as *turn and talk* to increase student engagement, so—no surprise—teachers would often say "Now, turn and talk to your neighbor . . ." as soon as I walked into the room, regardless of whether it was appropriate at that point in the lesson.

Of course, focused data collection can be of some value in specific situations—for example, identifying patterns of teacher behavior that could inform professional development decisions, or shadowing English learner students to identify ways to serve them more effectively (Ginsberg, 2012). Occasional student shadowing can be a valuable learning experience for leaders, but large-scale data collection conflicts with the goals of the high-performance instructional leadership model, which seeks to provide leaders with information that can lead to better discussions and better decisions.

Feedback-Focused Walkthroughs

Another popular model—perhaps the most widespread model in voluntary use—is the feedback-focused walkthrough, in which teachers receive brief suggestions for improvement based on a short observation. This model offers the strongest intuitive appeal and the most immediate payoff because the feedback teachers receive is the *low-hanging fruit* of improvement (Bambrick-Santoyo, 2012). Given suggestions and a modest degree of accountability, most teachers can make some improvements to their practice. This model is neither unreasonable nor wrongheaded; however, when taken to extremes, it can place needless strain on your time and your relationships with teachers.

Giving and receiving feedback is helpful for both of the individuals involved, and a high-feedback culture is good for everyone.

Under the best of circumstances, feedback-focused walkthroughs can lead to modest but continual improvements, as well as valuable professional learning for the instructional leader. Teacher coaching, in particular, is associated with student learning gains (Grissom et al., 2013). Giving and receiving feedback is helpful for both of the individuals involved, and a high-feedback culture is good for everyone. For new teachers, who may have multiple areas in which they can make rapid improvements, intensive feedback cycles can produce more substantial gains (Bambrick-Santoyo, 2012). The problem arises when educators push feedback-focused walkthroughs beyond the bounds of what they can reasonably accomplish; a law of diminishing returns applies to feedback. As teachers' experience and expertise grow, less and less low-hanging fruit remains, and the instructional leader faces the unenviable challenge of needing to become increasingly critical in order to provide feedback for improvement. The situation worsens when instructional leaders see their role as one of catching and correcting all of the mistakes teachers are making in their typical teaching practice—taking on too much of the responsibility for professional growth that teachers and other instructional leaders should share. Rather than trying to correct individual decisions, we should seek to elicit and raise the level of teachers' thinking about their instructional decision making through evidence-based conversations. Furthermore, we can often find the greatest leverage for improvement in schoolwide insights—such as patterns that we may need to address in professional development sessions for all staff—not in individual changes teachers make in response to feedback.

A more basic problem is perhaps the most commonly experienced flaw in feedback-focused walkthroughs: they're unpleasant, and as a result, instructional leaders rarely do them (Grissom et al., 2013). Teachers face uninvited (and seemingly unnecessary) criticism, and administrators must assume the role of critic. This dynamic exists even if it's masked by a high degree of professionalism. Teachers know they are required to "accept" feedback, even if they disagree with it, and supervisors know their presence is unwanted. The mandate to bring about continual improvement can propel the process only so far before resentment and avoidance set in.

Feedback-focused walkthroughs can also have unintended consequences. For example, teachers may learn to play the game of accepting feedback graciously in order to end the interaction as quickly as possible, without allowing the feedback to truly influence their thinking or practice. Given that the purpose of feedback is to improve teachers' thinking and instructional decision making (Danielson, 2015), this is a serious limitation. Administrators are playing the game, too, providing feedback just for the sake of having something to say—even if it's not helpful to the teacher. Over time, this can lead to an unfortunate cycle in which instructional leaders go to great lengths to give some sort of feedback, even when they know it is of poor quality, and teachers go to great lengths to pretend they value it. The more teachers pretend to benefit from feedback, the harder it is for instructional leaders to give truly useful feedback, and the cycle worsens—wasting everyone's time and resulting in no meaningful improvement.

Does feedback have any value at all? Under the right circumstances, yes. Feedback can be helpful when:

- The teacher requests feedback on a specific aspect of his or her practice
- The instructional leader has adequate time and expertise to observe and provide timely feedback on that specific aspect of the teacher's practice
- The instructional leader creates a sense of safety by separating the feedback and growth cycle from the formal evaluation process

These conditions are difficult for administrators to achieve on a consistent basis. Danielson (2015) notes that feedback can be validating and motivating for early career teachers, but for more experienced teachers, it "is even seen as a possible hindrance" (p. 10) to professional growth. It's not surprising, then, that instructional coaching has emerged as a powerful alternative to supervisory classroom walkthroughs.

Instructional Coaching

Many administrators aspire to serve, first and foremost, as instructional coaches for their teachers, and only secondarily as evaluators. This is an admirable mindset, and one that leads to greater mutual benefit from both formal observations and informal classroom visits. However, we should be clear that supervisors, strictly speaking, can never be true coaches, due to the structural power they wield over teachers (Knight, 2011). The power differential between teachers and administrators has the potential to overshadow the focus on growth with its emphasis on evaluation (Danielson, 2015). Coaching requires a commitment to the client's goals and a respect for confidentiality that shields the client from the potential negative consequences of taking risks. For example, a coach who is helping a teacher implement an ambitious new approach to project-based learning must refrain from filing negative reports if the teacher's early attempts are unsuccessful in order to avoid discouraging further efforts. An instructional leader who is also the teacher's evaluator can encourage risk taking but cannot promise to remain uninfluenced by what he or she sees in the classroom.

If you do serve as an instructional coach, you may find that the high-performance instructional leadership model is especially helpful for working with teachers who may be more defensive about their practice, thanks to its focus on evidence and shared criteria for quality. The coaching process can focus on the teacher's goals but stay rooted in evidence of what actually took place.

Keep in mind that I designed this model to generate decisional information, and while some of that information should be protected by the confidentiality requirements of the coaching relationship, instructional coaches should present other issues to administrative staff for their consideration. For example, if teachers routinely complain that it is difficult to teach within a less-than-ideal bell schedule, you can provide this information to the administrator responsible for the schedule and seek a change, rather than merely helping teachers cope with it.

The Downey Walkthrough

A well-regarded approach known as the Downey Walkthrough, or the Three-Minute Classroom Walkthrough, bears more similarity to the high-performance instructional leadership model than the others in this chapter (Downey, Steffy, English, Frase, & Poston, 2004). Carolyn J. Downey and her colleagues (2004) recommend visiting classrooms very briefly—for just two or three minutes—to look for instructional decisions that may be of interest and to gain a sense of students' orientation to their work. Because these visits are so brief, they can happen with great frequency, and because they usually involve no communication or follow-up with the teacher, they present relatively few barriers to implementation. Downey et al. (2004) recommend engaging teachers in reflective conversation "only when you know it will be received in a meaningful and timely manner" (p. 3), and taking only minimal notes in order to prompt recall of the most salient issues.

Compared to the Downey model, the high-performance instructional leadership model features a more consistent pattern of fewer, slightly longer visits each day, accompanied by more substantive and understanding-oriented, rather than coaching-oriented, conversations with teachers. Both models share a focus on instructional decision making rather than directive feedback. If you've been following the Downey model, you may find it relatively easy to transition to the high-performance instructional leadership model.

Learning Walks and Instructional Rounds

As they recognize the importance of spending time in classrooms, district- and system-level leaders are increasingly turning their attention to learning walks and instructional rounds (City, Elmore, Fiarman, & Teitel, 2009; Teitel, 2013). Though definitions and practices vary, *learning walks* usually involve groups of staff—including professionals other than teachers' direct supervisors—visiting classrooms together. In some cases, other teachers, parents, and students may also participate in learning walks. After a learning walk, the visiting team may debrief with or without the teachers it observed, and may or may not provide feedback.

The goal in all learning walk models is to learn from classroom practice, and this is an admirable goal.

The goal in all learning walk models is to learn from classroom practice, and this is an admirable goal. If you can organize a learning walk in your school or district—or better yet, schedule regular learning walks in each school—you are likely to find them valuable. Consider the following points.

‣ Learning walks should be explicitly nonevaluative—a team with very little context about a teacher's practice is not in a position to fairly evaluate that practice (City et al., 2009).

- Teachers should receive advance notice that the team may visit during the learning walk, simply as a professional courtesy and to avoid wasting time if, for example, students will be taking a test during the given time slot.
- The team's focus should remain on its own learning, not providing feedback to teachers or evaluating their practice, and it should communicate this focus clearly to teachers in advance.
- All teachers who are observed during the learning walk should receive some type of encouraging comment or acknowledgement, such as a thank-you note.
- While the learning walk team may generate questions for inquiry and discussion (such as, "Did the teacher consider doing X instead of Y?"), no one should pose these questions to teachers on the spot in order to avoid putting them on the defensive.

A more specific and well-defined model that has gained traction, driven by the work of Elizabeth City, Richard Elmore, and their colleagues at the Harvard Graduate School of Education, is the practice of *instructional rounds* (City et al., 2009). In this model, central office leaders take a purposeful and systematic approach to learning walks, seeking to glean organizational insights from their time in classrooms. In the instructional rounds model, the focus is on system and cross-system learning and decision making more than individual learning. Because the individual instructional leader and teacher are not the primary focus, instructional rounds may not include feedback to the teacher or a conversation with the teacher.

In contrast, the high-performance instructional leadership model is designed to provide an individual leader with a deep understanding of each teacher's practice and decision making through repeated observations and conversations. Given these distinct purposes, you may find instructional rounds to be a useful complement to the high-performance instructional leadership model.

Hybrid Models

You will no doubt use a combination of these models under various circumstances, such as when you visit classrooms with a leader you work with, and when you conduct formal evaluations of the teachers or leaders you supervise. Follow the high-performance instructional leadership model closely, and modify it only when you have a specific reason for doing so. For example, when you typically visit classrooms, you may take notes and have a follow-up conversation with the teacher later in the day. During a learning walk with your peers and supervisors, though, you may choose to visit each classroom without taking notes and chart your observations as a group later. Regardless of your approach, strive to match your process to your goals and avoid unintended consequences by preparing carefully.

Day 3 Action Challenge: Review Your Instructional Leadership Models

Make a list of the instructional leadership and supervision processes you currently use in your school. You may want to consider the following questions for reflection as you review the models you're currently using.

- ‣ How do your current instructional leadership processes overlap and interact with one another?
- ‣ How do they impact teachers, and how do teachers perceive them?
- ‣ If you were to implement the high-performance instructional leadership model with perfect fidelity, how would that impact the other models in use in your school or district?

4

Conducting Your First Two Cycles of Visits

Now that we've explored the high-performance instructional leadership model in depth, compared it to other models, and identified the role it can play in your larger work, it's time to take action. In this chapter, you'll learn how to plan your first two cycles of classroom visits—two rounds of visiting every teacher you supervise. It's critical to begin with the full cycle in mind rather than start to visit classrooms without a solid plan, because how you start determines how successful you will be—which, in turn, will determine whether you abandon your attempts or turn them into a powerful habit. This chapter will help you develop a realistic plan for your visits, as well as set expectations and communicate your intentions to teachers. We'll then discuss how to conduct your first cycle of visits and highlight how this process will develop into your second cycle.

Consider Planning Issues

If you're a school administrator, there's a good chance you've already resolved and attempted to make regular visits to classrooms a core element of your leadership practice. If you're like most administrators, though, your attempts have been short lived and less impactful than you'd have liked. Using the strategies in this book, every administrator can—and should—visit classrooms upwards of five hundred times per year (three classrooms a day for most—if not all—days of the school year), but make no mistake: it's a challenge. And as with any challenge, success requires a solid plan.

There are two key planning issues to consider. First, you'll want to develop a realistic schedule that creates time for classroom visits, and a plan to handle the additional work they create. Second, you'll want to plan what expectations you'll communicate to staff about your high-performance instructional leadership visits, as well as how and when you'll communicate about them.

Develop a Realistic Schedule and Plan

If you're excited about the idea of getting into classrooms more, you may be tempted to set an unrealistic goal such as visiting every classroom every day. Instead, let your commitment and enthusiasm spur you toward realistic planning and diligent follow-through. On the other hand, don't aim too low or try to ease into the habit; like medicine, classroom visits require a certain dose to have any meaningful impact, so if you decide to visit only one classroom a day, you won't have a noticeable impact on learning and won't get the positive feedback that is essential for forming habits.

Plan to visit three classrooms per day, every day. If you share teacher evaluation responsibilities with other administrators in your school, plan to visit only the teachers you evaluate. Most administrators evaluate approximately thirty teachers, so making three visits per day should take you to every classroom every two weeks or so. If you supervise a large number of teachers, you may not make it around to each teacher quite as often, but having a sustainable, consistent habit is the goal, and three visits per day seems to strike a reasonable balance between practicality and frequency.

Plan to visit three classrooms per day, every day.

You may be concerned about the time it will take to visit three classrooms per day, but once you get started, you'll find that you can recoup this time in a variety of ways. Many administrators have reported to me that they saw a drop in office referrals when they began a regular habit of visiting classrooms—perhaps because teachers are more able to handle minor discipline issues when administrators regularly visit their classrooms.

One of the most common complaints of administrators is that emergencies interfere with visiting classrooms as planned. If you know there's a good chance that your plans will be disrupted, build a few extra blocks into your schedule. Your visits should be spread out throughout the day and, whenever possible, adjacent to other events on your calendar. For example, you may want to visit classrooms on the way to an existing meeting or scheduled supervision duty, as it's easier to leave the office a few minutes early than to interrupt a block of focused office work.

To minimize the chance of disruption, schedule short visits throughout the day, rather than one long, continuous block of time. If you schedule a ninety-minute midmorning block for classroom visits, a single interruption could derail your plans. Instead, schedule shorter time slots throughout the day, and schedule more than you need. If your school day is divided into class periods, schedule one visit during each period, so you can get around to more classes. You may find it easier to get into classrooms in the morning, but interruptions will often force you to use the afternoon time slots. Additional suggestions for scheduling are included in chapter 6 (page 53).

You'll also want to consider the order in which you will visit classrooms. It's helpful to visit teams or departments back to back, for several reasons. First, it's harder to miss someone when you're observing an entire team or department in just a day or two. It will be tempting to first visit the teachers who are the friendliest, highest performing, and physically closest to the office. This means you'll wait until the end of the cycle to see the toughest-to-visit teachers, which creates a growing incentive to abandon your efforts. Instead of saving the toughest teachers for last, develop a systematic plan: Which grade levels or departments will you visit first? Plan to visit each team in succession, and continue the same order through your second cycle in order to equally space the visits.

Second, you'll learn much more about the curriculum, shared practices, and assessments that a team or department uses when you visit every member of the group in rapid succession. Once, I observed a first-grade mathematics lesson that made no sense to me as a new principal still becoming familiar with the district's new mathematics curriculum. At first, I mentally blamed the teacher for failing to plan a coherent lesson. When I visited the classroom next door, though, I saw the rest of the lesson—taught by an equally effective teacher—and it all made sense. Because I became better informed before speaking with the teacher, I avoided a serious misstep. The more context you can gain by visiting other teachers in the same grade or department, the richer your conversations with teachers can be.

The more context you can gain by visiting other teachers in the same grade or department, the richer your conversations with teachers can be.

Third, you'll be able to draw more direct comparisons between classrooms, which will increase the quality of your feedback. When you see the pros and cons of different approaches side by side—even if you're not going straight from one class to another but merely visiting on the same day—you can more easily provide useful recommendations to teachers and engage in more productive conversations about learning.

Fourth, you'll find that teachers will immediately check in with their closest colleagues when you start visiting classrooms. If they feel you're singling out or targeting them with increased scrutiny, they'll naturally become more fearful and defensive. For this reason, you may want to visit all the members of a team in rapid succession, so when they compare notes, they'll know you are not singling them out. You'll also want to be sure to visit every teacher once before visiting any teacher a second time. This is an essential aspect of communicating positive intent and minimizing teachers' anxiety about your increased presence in classrooms, which we now explore in greater depth.

Set Expectations and Communicate Your Intentions

For your first cycle, it's best to just start visiting classrooms without any kind of formal announcement. The more you remain low-key about your classroom visits, the less likely you are to spark mass resistance, which is important if the level of trust isn't especially high in your school. Your visits will surprise teachers, and it's your job during this first cycle to ensure that it's a pleasant surprise. While it might seem preferable to make a general announcement before beginning your visits, an announcement will trigger a range of reactions based on teachers' previous experience with administrators, and it's best to simply allow your visits to speak for themselves.

Your goal should be to gain teachers' confidence that you aren't visiting to conduct "gotcha" inspections and catch teachers at their worst but instead to listen, learn, converse with them, and become a more effective leader. The easiest way to send the right message and avoid triggering fears of a "gotcha" observation is to simply drop by, pay attention without taking notes, show interest in the lesson, and say something nice before you leave. We explore additional strategies for your first round of visits in the following section.

Your goal should be to gain teachers' confidence that you aren't visiting to conduct "gotcha" inspections and catch teachers at their worst but instead to listen, learn, converse with them, and become a more effective leader.

Another question at the top of teachers' minds will be the purpose of your visits and what role, if any, they'll play in your evaluations of teachers' performance. While it may be tempting to state unequivocally that your visits are nonevaluative, a caution is in order. If you are the evaluator of record, you can't ensure that your firsthand classroom observations, whether formal or informal, will not influence your final evaluations. Instead of focusing on the question of whether your visits are evaluative or not, emphasize your purpose in visiting—to listen, to learn, and to lead more effectively. If a teacher asks you directly whether your visits are evaluative, you can respond that they're not formal observations and you won't write them up as such, but that final evaluations are summative and based on your full body of evidence about teachers' practice. You can also emphasize that the more you're in classrooms, the more likely you are to have a fair portrait of teachers' practice (Marshall, 2013).

Conduct Your First Cycle of Visits

In your first cycle of visits, which should begin before you make any formal announcement to staff, you'll want to avoid heavy feedback. Focus on listening, and make only encouraging, observational comments to teachers. Simply walk in unobtrusively, with a friendly look on your face, and pay attention to what's going on. Don't bring a laptop or take any notes. Participate if appropriate. Don't interrupt or interrogate students. If the teacher stops the class to welcome you, encourage him or her to proceed with the lesson. Focus on building rapport by listening and learning and having a pleasant conversation as time allows.

Stay for five to ten minutes, and before you leave, offer your thanks and compliment the teacher on something positive from the lesson. Don't try to get into a deep conversation or offer constructive criticism; the goal at this stage is to build a foundation of trust. Make your visit a positive experience for everyone involved—even you. That way, you're more likely to form and sustain the habit over the long term, and teachers are less likely to resist your visits.

As word gets out that you're visiting classrooms, you'll want to acknowledge your new practice in a brief announcement in a meeting, a newsletter, or an all-staff email. Wait to make this announcement until after you've visited everyone once, so no one feels targeted or left out. In this announcement, state that your goal is to simply visit classrooms more often to become a more effective leader and to learn more about the great things that are taking place in your school. You don't need to give too many details, but again, be careful not to promise that your visits are nonevaluative; simply state that your goal is to learn and increase your effectiveness as an instructional leader. Teachers' concerns will be kept to a minimum if you visit members of each team in rapid succession following this protocol.

Look Ahead to Your Second Cycle of Visits

Your second cycle of visits will be similar to the first. After you've visited each teacher once, simply start again at the top of your list, and visit classrooms again in the same order. In this second cycle, you'll want to raise the bar by striving to have a substantive, evidence-based conversation with each teacher. Keep it positive and continue to focus on building trust and rapport. Don't take notes or provide suggestions for improvement; simply pay attention while you're observing. The best way to improve your visits in this second cycle is simply to notice more, communicate more, and ask better questions; there's no need to become critical.

Review the high-performance instructional leadership model in chapter 2 (page 15), and strive to refine your approach in your second cycle so your visits remain frequent, brief, conversation oriented, and open ended, but become more substantive, evidence based, and criterion referenced.

Day 4 Action Challenge: Visit Your First Three Classrooms

Visit three classrooms. Don't ease into it with just one visit, and don't overcommit; three is a doable and ideal number of visits per day. Stay in each classroom for a few minutes, and then have a brief conversation with the teacher before you leave, or later in the day if necessary. Don't worry about coming up with suggestions—just chat briefly, say something nice, and thank the teacher for taking the time to speak with you.

After your visits, jot down some notes about the experience.

- How were you received?
- What message do you think your presence in the room sent to teachers and students?
- Did you encounter any resistance? If so, what changes might reduce resistance in future visits to the same teacher or teachers?
- What do you think you might say in your announcement to staff after you complete your first cycle of visits?

5

Thinking Ahead to
Your Third Cycle of Visits

Let's take a moment to look ahead and see how the high-performance instructional leadership model will help you deepen your practice of visiting classrooms in the coming weeks. The first round of visits focuses on making a positive impression to help teachers become comfortable with your increased presence in their classrooms. In your second round, you'll start to directly root your conversations with teachers in specific evidence, particularly evidence pertaining to the instructional framework you identified in chapter 2 (page 15). In these first two cycles, conversations with teachers should remain completely positive unless you've encountered a major problem that you need to address.

In your third cycle of visits, you'll want to fully enact the high-performance instructional leadership model. This chapter will help you prepare your staff, develop a note-taking and note-sharing process, further develop your instructional framework, and integrate classroom visits into your daily habits. By doing so, it will help you set yourself and your staff up for success from the outset, so the process of visiting classrooms and talking with teachers starts to yield benefits and becomes a permanent habit in your instructional leadership repertoire.

Keep an Open Mind

By the time you've visited every classroom twice, you may start to identify patterns that lead you to certain areas of focus that you want to investigate more carefully. For example, you may notice a wide variation in teachers' approaches to using questioning strategies with students, so you may want to pay special attention to such strategies in your third round of visits. Two notes of caution are in order.

First, resist the tendency to inflate the validity of any trends you identify in your first two rounds. After visiting three classrooms a day for a few weeks, you'll know far more than most instructional leaders about what's taking place in classrooms, and it will be tempting to believe that you're ready to roll out an action plan in response to what you've seen. However, you'll have seen a very small proportion of the total instruction that's taken place. The information you'll gain has enormous value, but you should not treat it as a scientific or representative sample; it's based on just a few minutes in each classroom and very little substantive conversation with teachers. In your third cycle, commit to having more in-depth, evidence-based, and framework-linked conversations with teachers. This will help you draw more accurate conclusions and develop a deeper understanding of each teacher's opportunities for growth.

In your third cycle, commit to having more in-depth, evidence-based, and framework-linked conversations with teachers.

Second, be mindful of the fact that when you visit classrooms, teachers change their behavior compared to when you aren't in the room—in other words, there's an observer effect. Your schedule is also likely constrained by existing patterns in the day (such as the lunch schedule and teachers' prep periods), so your visits throughout each class and throughout the day aren't randomly distributed. You'll gain valuable decisional information, but it's far from fully representative data about what's taking place in classrooms, so take it with a grain of salt when deciding on next steps.

Prepare Staff for Your Third Round of Visits

As you wrap up your second round of visits, announce to your staff that you've been enjoying your visits to classrooms and that you intend to deepen the practice. Explain that your visits would be more informative and helpful to you as a leader if you had the chance to talk in greater depth with teachers after you visit. Then, reveal that you'll be taking notes about what you see in classrooms and that you'll be sharing and discussing these notes with each teacher after each visit. If you plan to email your notes to teachers, explain your purpose and clarify your expectations for whether teachers need to reply. By setting expectations with your entire staff at once, you'll avoid making individuals feel targeted or harassed.

Take Notes and Share Them With Teachers

Ideally, you'll want to have brief, face-to-face conversations with teachers after each visit. Since these conversations can't always happen immediately, it's important to reassure teachers that you aren't compiling secret dossiers on them—which will be a legitimate concern if you suddenly appear, laptop in hand, and start taking copious notes. If you've explained in advance that you'll be sharing these notes with the teacher immediately, you will have assuaged many of these potential fears.

Ideally, you'll want to have brief, face-to-face conversations with teachers after each visit.

You may want to take a detailed running record of what you notice in the classroom, using low-inference, descriptive notes with timestamps. Or, you may prefer to jot down less detailed notes, simply capturing enough information to inform your subsequent conversation. For example, you may write "9:42—Students working independently on practice problems; teacher circulating to monitor their work. Asks one student 'How did you get that answer?'" followed by "9:47—Student asks 'Is this like what we did yesterday?'" Whatever your style, strive to capture verbatim teacher and student quotes, and describe clearly what the teacher and students are doing. Don't include commentary, compliments, or suggestions—your notes should be purely descriptive. You may interpret your notes later when writing a formal evaluation, but for now, description is all you need. You don't need to write down everything that happens, but be sure that what you record is as descriptive as possible.

You have several options for the form your notes take when you deliver them; the simplest way to share notes with teachers is to simply send them an email, which requires no other apps or special technology. If your school uses an evaluation or feedback management system or app, you may want to send your notes through that system for consistency and convenience.

Many instructional leaders have told me they prefer to take handwritten notes and that they believe teachers find this practice less intimidating than taking typewritten notes. While individual preferences will vary, keep in mind that handwritten notes are significantly more difficult to share with teachers, because you'll want to keep a copy for your records so you can easily access your notes later. You can take a photo of handwritten notes with your phone, but if these photos aren't organized carefully, they'll be of limited use. Transparency about what you are writing down is essential for building trust in this process, so it's best to immediately share your notes electronically, rather than photograph or make a copy of hard-to-read handwritten notes later.

Forge Stronger Links to Your Instructional Framework

Your third round of visits is a key point in your instructional leadership trajectory. Don't miss this chance to intensify your focus on the language and criteria of your instructional framework. Since instructional frameworks often serve as evaluation tools, you might be tempted to use your framework to evaluate what you see during your third round of visits, but that's not our approach in the high-performance instructional leadership model.

Instead of using your instructional framework to evaluate the instruction you see, use it to expand and sharpen your vocabulary for talking about teaching and learning. You may not even need to explicitly mention the framework in any given conversation; as its language becomes second nature to you and your staff, it can make a difference whether it's identified as a *participant* in the conversation or not. For example, you may choose to adopt Charlotte Danielson's (2007) *Enhancing Professional Practice: A Framework for Teaching* as part of your instructional framework. Danielson (2007) outlines twenty-two components of professional teacher practice in four broad domains: (1) planning and preparation, (2) the classroom environment, (3) instruction, and (4) professional responsibilities. Each of the twenty-two components includes four leveled descriptors of practice: *unsatisfactory, basic, proficient,* and *distinguished.* If you visit a classroom during a lively class discussion, you might quickly glance at your framework to review its language about questioning techniques and managing class discussions. You might notice, for example, that Danielson's (2007) domain 3, component B, is *using questioning and discussion techniques,* and that the *distinguished* column uses the phrases "challenge students cognitively" and "students . . . challenge one another's thinking." Even if you don't make explicit reference to these criteria in your notes or conversation, you can strive to use vocabulary consistent with your framework, and to address the issues that are most salient according to the framework.

However, if you explicitly position it as the authoritative standard on professional practice, your framework can help you have more rigorous, yet less adversarial, conversations with teachers. This keeps your conversation from becoming a battle of wills or competing education philosophies and allows you to focus squarely on the evidence and what it means relative to the framework's criteria. To make reference to your instructional framework, you might use sentence structures such as the following.

- "I was looking over our framework's standards for [criterion], and I noticed that [evidence]."
- "Our framework talks about setting instructional outcomes in [criterion], and I noticed that [evidence]. How would you situate that evidence within the performance descriptors?"
- "Looking at the criteria from our framework, what stands out to you from [evidence]?"

Remember an important distinction: you should avoid any attempt to rate or score teachers based on individual pieces of evidence, because teacher evaluation criteria are for evaluating the teacher's overall practice, not specific instances. Avoid statements such as, "You did [evidence], so you're *proficient* on our framework." The evidence may align with descriptors of a particular level of performance, but the evidence itself is not a discrete performance that you can score. Instead, the evidence provides a basis for triangulating expectations—it allows teachers and instructional leaders to explore their mutual understandings of the criteria and the pattern that may be developing over time. But we need more than a single piece of evidence—it's only after a pattern has emerged that you can conduct a valid evaluation of the teacher's practice.

Finally, when you're discussing the evidence and the instructional framework, the teacher should do most of the talking. One strategy you can use to keep the conversation going, without taking too heavy a role in guiding it, is to ask *broken questions*. For example, you might say, "So, looking at standard 7 and thinking about what we saw today, what do you see as . . ." and simply trail off. Don't ask a specific question; just suggest a direction and let the teacher run with it: "Yeah, I wanted students to have the chance to discuss Maya Angelou's life experiences and how they shaped her writing . . ." Or you might cite a particular incident you observed and let the teacher interpret it: "So I noticed that group 3 got into a discussion of earthquakes. How did that . . ." and the teacher might chime in with "I know it seems a little bit off-topic, but I was pleased that they made the connection." Such questions may sound awkward in writing, but in verbal conversation it's perfectly natural for the teacher to jump in and pick up where you leave off. Broken questions can allow you to inquire into specific issues without framing them as either positive or negative—so you can avoid putting the teacher on the defensive.

Experience the Rewards of the Classroom Habit

As you enter your third round of visits, you'll find countless reasons to let your daily practice of visiting classrooms slip. There will be a holiday break, you'll be out of the building for professional development, or half the school will be on a field trip. Or perhaps you'll just get busier than usual. Regardless of the factors standing in your way, stick with it. You've experienced success in visiting three classrooms a day, and you've helped your teachers warm up to your visits and the subsequent conversations.

In the first two cycles, the benefits of your high-performance instructional leadership practice will be mostly interpersonal; you'll be more present and visible to your teachers, and you'll have more chances to acknowledge their work. As you begin your third cycle of visits, you'll start to notice a profound shift. You'll know dramatically more about what's going on in every classroom. Though your visits will continue to be brief, you'll develop a deeper understanding of your school's curriculum, as well as each teacher's strengths and weaknesses. You'll gain a greater sense of the key opportunities and challenges your school faces, and this will enable you to make better decisions about how to allocate scarce resources such as time and money.

The immediate and ongoing benefit of implementing the high-performance instructional leadership model is that it continually provides what leaders need most: information to inform decisions. This information will continue to flow to you, and the more consistently you visit classrooms, the more clarity you'll gain about what to do with it.

It's essential at this point to not allow classroom visits to become something you do only when time allows. Take control of your schedule and *make* time. Make it a habit to visit three classrooms a day, and you'll wonder how you ever made decisions without doing so.

> *The immediate and ongoing benefit of implementing the high-performance instructional leadership model is that it continually provides what leaders need most: information to inform decisions.*

Day 5 Action Challenge: Visit a Team

Today, visit three members of a department, grade level, or other team. As you continue your daily rounds, strive to visit members of teams back-to-back.

You may want to consider the following questions for reflection.

- What am I learning that I wouldn't have noticed if I hadn't visited members of the same team back-to-back?
- Which teachers did I feel the most reluctant to visit?
- What similarities and differences between teachers stood out most as I visited members of the same team?

Continue to focus on relationship and rapport building.

Always have a brief conversation with each teacher after you visit, even if it's after school or the following day. Talking with every teacher you visit is essential for preventing any fear or suspicion about what you noticed during the visit. If you need to set aside time during a teacher's prep period to ensure that you have a chance to chat, mark it on your calendar.

As you progress through the book, continue visiting three classrooms a day. Keep track of your visits, and make sure you aren't skipping anyone; in the next two cycles, you'll visit teachers in the same order.

WEEK 2

High-Performance Habits

It's not enough to *start* visiting classrooms; our goal is to develop a consistent, sustainable *habit* over the long term. While simply prioritizing classroom visits—and postponing other work—may be effective in the short term, most leaders need more systematic productivity techniques to stay current on other work while getting into three classrooms a day. When you reach your third cycle of classroom visits and strive to make your conversations with teachers more substantive and impactful, the time management challenge will grow. In this section, we'll explore high-performance habits that will help you sustain your efforts to visit classrooms every day.

6

Making Time
to Visit Classrooms

Now that you have a solid plan for visiting classrooms, the greatest remaining barrier is time. You'll never find unused time in your day, no matter how organized you are; you'll have to create time by carving it out of your calendar. Yet it's not enough to simply prioritize and avoid other realities in order to get into classrooms. In this chapter, we'll explore specific strategies for scheduling your high-performance instructional leadership visits each day.

Parkinson's law states that "work expands to fill the time available for its completion" (Parkinson, 1957, p. 3). In other words, you'll never *not* use all of the time available to you each day; the only question is *how* you'll use it. This chapter will help you reduce interruptions caused by emergencies, create time through self-discipline, schedule short time blocks for classroom visits, and keep track of your visits. These scheduling techniques can free up all the time you need for classroom visits—and more.

Reduce Interruptions From Emergencies

If you're like most administrators, you probably spend several hours each day dealing with interruptions and emergencies of various types. Some of these legitimately need your attention, while others could be handled without you or postponed to another time that wouldn't disrupt your calendar.

Let's consider interruptions that come from issues that do require your attention, but not immediately. Many of the "emergencies" that interrupt administrators throughout the day could, in reality, receive attention five or ten minutes later without any negative consequences. When I ask school leaders to define what constitutes an emergency, I sometimes hear answers like "if there's blood" or "if it's a safety issue." Consider, though, how these scenarios go when you're absent for the day. Are you the nurse? Are bleeding students going untreated when you're absent? Are other staff members incapable of responding to safety issues? Of course not, and whatever occurs when you're off-campus can also occur when you're in classrooms. When other staff members consider an issue to be an emergency worth interrupting you about, they usually feel they should at least notify you about the issue and possibly consult with you about what to do. Typically, though, this can wait five to ten minutes.

Sit down with your office staff and make a list of true emergencies that justify interrupting your classroom visits, for example, a lockdown or evacuation. If an issue can wait a few minutes, it shouldn't warrant interrupting you. Discuss how office staff can respond to the typical near-emergency issues that arise in your school, including what to do when you're not immediately available.

You can either delegate near-emergencies or put them off until you return to the office. For example, a discipline referral is not usually a true emergency; students can typically wait fifteen minutes to speak with you, and in fact, it may be preferable to give them a few minutes to cool down. It may not be appropriate for another staff member to handle student discipline issues or confidential staff concerns. On the other hand, someone with the authority to initiate a lockdown or evacuation should always be available. A serious medical emergency may warrant an interruption, but you should discuss with your office staff what types of situations you're comfortable hearing about after they're handled and which situations you want to know about immediately.

Create Time Through Self-Discipline

The foundation of time management is self-discipline. It does no good to plan your schedule for the day, eliminate interruptions, and give strict instructions to your office staff if you aren't going to follow your calendar. For most school leaders, this is a formidable challenge—leaders are conditioned to respond to emerging situations (Mintzberg, 1973), and we learn not to be too disappointed if we're unable to achieve everything we've planned for the day. But without committing to making a plan for daily classroom visits and sticking to it, you reduce your efforts to wishful thinking.

The foundation of time management is self-discipline.

While we may be unable to fit in everything we'd like, no daily habit is more essential than spending time visiting classrooms and talking with teachers. High-performance instructional leadership must be our top priority. And when it's not possible to visit classrooms—due to meetings, crises, or other factors—we must continue to adhere to our written plans for the day as closely as possible. If you're forced to adjust, don't scrap your plans; modify them. If your schedule changes, don't abandon your calendar for the day; update it. Always make sure you're doing what's on your calendar, and always make sure what you're doing is on your calendar. This honesty with yourself—and deference to your calendar—will serve you well as you face tough choices about how to spend your time.

Self-discipline starts at the planning stage: take a few minutes each day to plan your work for the next day. By deciding what to work on in advance, you'll be more realistic about your overall workload, energy level, and schedule for the day, and you'll enjoy a greater ability to protect time for classroom visits.

Schedule Short Time Blocks for Visiting Classrooms

When it's time to schedule specific blocks of time to visit classrooms, you'll want to schedule brief, frequent blocks on your calendar rather than long, continuous blocks. The longer the block of time is, the more likely it is that daily happenings will interrupt you—and the harder it'll be to reschedule it for later. When working with groups of administrators on their classroom visit schedules, I've often found that they attempt to set aside an entire morning, or even an entire day, to visit classrooms. Schedule shorter blocks, and you'll have fewer difficulties making it into classrooms. You can schedule a block as short as ten minutes, or as long as your schedule and the realities of the school day allow, but I generally recommend keeping these blocks to thirty minutes or less. You may still want to schedule some blocks that are long enough to visit an entire team or department during the same portion of the day, but you may also want to take advantage of built-in breaks—for example, you may go to a classroom, then supervise a passing period or recess, then go straight to another classroom.

You'll also want to schedule more blocks than you need. For example, to visit three teachers per day, you may want to schedule five or six possible times on your calendar to account for inevitable interruptions. The more frequently you get interrupted, the more additional blocks you'll want to schedule. When one of these blocks arrives, don't treat it as optional just because you have extra blocks scheduled for later in the day—unless you've already hit your goal for the day, go immediately to the next classroom on your list.

For example, let's say John is an elementary principal whose school day runs from 8:00 a.m. to 3:00 p.m. Students come and go to specialists' classes, recess, and lunch at various times throughout the day, and John covers several recess and lunch duties throughout the week. None of these duties occur between 8:00 and 9:15 a.m., so John tries to visit an entire grade-level team between 8:45 and 9:15 a.m. daily. This gives him time to respond to any parent concerns and phone calls, and get a bit of office work done before he heads out to visit classrooms. Because John's school has few discipline issues in the morning, he's usually not interrupted during this thirty-minute block, so he can almost always complete two or three classroom visits before heading to his first recess duty.

John covers K–2 lunch duty daily starting at 11:15, so he schedules a classroom visit block at 11:00. This requires John to stop what he's working on in the office a few minutes earlier, but the disruption is minimal since he's able to work in the office from 9:15 to 11:00. Because

K–2 students are preparing to transition to lunch at that time, John usually visits third-, fourth-, and fifth-grade classes, who don't go to lunch until 11:45.

In the afternoon, John usually deals with a few discipline issues, so he knows he'll need to plan more blocks than he'll actually need, to account for interruptions. John schedules fifteen-minute blocks from 1:20 to 1:35 and 2:25 to 2:40, adjacent to his afternoon recess duties, and he expects to visit classrooms (or catch up with teachers he visited earlier in the day, in case he didn't get a chance to talk with them) during at least one of those two blocks. School is over at 3:00 p.m., but John usually doesn't plan any visits between 2:40 and 3:00; however, he can drop into classrooms or catch up with teachers during this time if he wants to.

With this schedule, John can often reach his goal of three classroom visits per day during the morning block alone. However, if he has a meeting or interruption during that time, he still has ample opportunity in his calendar to reach his goal later in the day. He also gets to visit classes at different times of day, so he doesn't always observe the same subject when he visits a particular teacher. He can check in frequently with the office, and can still get plenty of office work done in between classroom visits.

Now we'll consider another example—let's say Susan is a high school principal who shares evaluation duties with two assistant principals. She wants to observe the teachers she evaluates at different times of day, and wants to make sure she has flexibility to attend her district's frequent off-campus meetings and still reach her goal of three class visits per day.

Susan's school has a six-period day, with three overlapping lunch periods. She and her assistant principals arrange their schedules so one administrator is in the office, one in the lunchroom, and one in classrooms during each lunch period. With this arrangement, she's able to visit classes that overlap with other teachers' lunch periods. Her school doesn't have recess, but she wants to make sure she can visit classes during any period with minimal disruption, so she decides to schedule a class visit block during every period. She only uses half of these blocks on any given day, but she finds that her high rate of interruptions due to emergencies and district meetings makes it essential to schedule six visits a day in order to consistently accomplish three.

Your own specific duties, staffing patterns, and school schedule will determine when you're able to schedule your classroom visits; what matters is that you create a viable schedule that will allow you, like John and Susan, to accomplish three visits per day, every day.

Schedule Visiting Blocks Based on Interruptions

Plan your classroom visit schedule based on how often you get interrupted. The formula to use is as follows.

**Number of desired visits per day ÷ Success rate =
Number of needed blocks**

For example, if you get interrupted 50 percent of the time when you attempt to visit classrooms and succeed 50 percent of the time, consider the following.

3 visits per day ÷ 0.5 success rate = 6 blocks per day

Schedule these six blocks on your calendar and consistently succeed in getting into classrooms during 50 percent of these blocks, and you'll be on track.

If you get interrupted two-thirds of the time and only succeed one-third of the time, the calculation would be as follows.

3 visits per day ÷ 0.33 success rate = 9 blocks per day

If, on the other hand, you can adhere to your schedule 80 percent of the time, you'll only need the following.

3 visits per day ÷ 0.8 success rate = 3.75 blocks per day

When the answer isn't a whole number, simply round up—in the last example, you'd need four blocks per day to reach your target consistently.

Coordinate and Track Your Visits

It's essential to keep track, from day one, of which teachers you've visited and on what dates. If you don't keep track, you'll systematically over-visit the friendliest, closest, and most competent teachers, and you'll unwittingly tend to avoid teachers who are farther away, less receptive to your visits and feedback, or struggling.

You can keep a list of all staff, but you may also want to get your administrative assistant or technology involved. A variety of electronic apps, such as Repertoire and TeachBoost, can help you keep track of your classroom visits and direct you to the next teacher in your rotation. If you prefer a low-tech solution, you can use a stack of notecards—one per teacher—to keep you on track. Each day, have your administrative assistant give you the top three cards from the stack. Check the names on these cards against your master schedule, and pick a scheduled block that matches each teacher's schedule so you don't attempt to visit during a teacher's prep period. As you visit each teacher, write the date of your visit on the notecard, and then return it to your administrative assistant, who will put it on the bottom of the stack. This simple system will ensure that you neither avoid the "tougher" teachers, nor over-visit the "easier" teachers. If a teacher is absent or otherwise unavailable, simply put his or her card back on top of the stack for tomorrow.

Self-discipline is critical when it comes to keeping your visits in order. Resist the temptation to skip around through your list, and always be sure to circle back to any teachers you miss due to absences.

Day 6 Action Challenge: Schedule Your Classroom Visit Blocks

Use the formula provided in this chapter to calculate how many blocks per day you'll need to reach your target of three classrooms per day (see Schedule Visiting Blocks Based on Interruptions, page 58). Examine your school's master schedule and your calendar, and schedule these blocks on your calendar. Use your electronic calendar's recurring appointment feature to make these blocks a permanent part of your calendar. If your school has a varied schedule from day to day, you may find it easier to schedule your blocks on a weekly basis.

Determine how you'll keep track of which teachers you've visited already and which teachers to visit next. Decide on a technology solution, or create a low-tech system by writing each teacher's name on a notecard and giving the stack to your administrative assistant. You may want to consider the following questions for reflection.

- What times of day am I most likely to avoid classrooms?

- What times of day am I least likely to be interrupted?

- How can I make office staff feel more supported in handling minor emergencies?

7

Keeping Your Communication Channels Under Control

While time is always scarce, it's possible—for every leader, nearly every day—to devote substantial time to our core work of instructional leadership. On days in which we don't get into classrooms, it's often not because time was in short supply, but because other aspects of our work consume our mental bandwidth. If, at the end of the school day, you look back and consider how you spent your time, it's often not hard to find times when you could have visited classrooms. When we're distracted by everything else that we could be doing, we simply won't get around to as many classrooms as we'd like.

To reach your goal and develop a consistent habit, then, you must free your mind from the stress and distractions that come from disorganization and uncertainty about what's waiting in your inbox, on your desk, and on your to-do list. You certainly don't have to *do* all of the work that's waiting for you before you can get out of the office; that would make it impossible to ever make it into classrooms. But it helps enormously to be *current*—to know what work is waiting for you back in the office and on your electronic devices, because you've processed, prioritized, and organized it. In this chapter, you'll learn how to stay current, streamline your communication channels, reduce non-emergency interruptions, process what is in your inboxes, and decide what you can defer.

Stay Current

If you have two hundred unread emails from the past two weeks, you aren't current—you don't know what's waiting for you, so you don't have a realistic assessment of how much work time those two hundred emails represent. If your desk is cluttered with documents and sticky notes, you don't know which unfinished projects have looming deadlines, and you can't effectively plan how you'll use your time. If you haven't checked voicemail in two days, you don't know what crises may be brewing. In all cases, a failure to stay current creates a sense of uncertainty and anxiety about whether it's advisable to get into classrooms.

The work waiting in your inbox, on your desk, and in your voicemail is usually less important than the work of visiting classrooms. It's sometimes quite urgent, sometimes quite important, and does need to be dealt with, but you should make decisions about how to spend your time based on up-to-date knowledge, priorities, and plans—not based on fear. Fear-driven work tends to be frantic, inconsistent, and rushed. Instead, empower yourself to make good prioritization and scheduling decisions with the whole picture in mind by getting current.

Streamline Your Information Sources

Your work doesn't arrive neatly packaged in a consistent format like tasks on a clipboard; it arrives through a wide range of media, in a wide range of formats, in a number of different inboxes. The more inboxes you have and the less clear you are on which inboxes are currently holding unprocessed obligations, the more anxiety you'll experience, and the harder it will be to get current so you can get into classrooms (Allen, 2015).

At a minimum, you probably have an email inbox, a physical mailbox or an inbox tray on your desk, and a voicemail inbox on your phone. You also likely have a method of tracking your own ideas and requests that people make of you in person; when I began my career as an administrator, before smartphones were ubiquitous, I used a pocket-sized notebook to keep track of anything I needed to do. You may also have a learning management system, two-way radio, social media platforms, and other channels of communication that generate potential work that you must track and complete.

Regardless of the specific tools you use, strive to minimize the number of inboxes containing action items by routing tasks into a few central locations. For example, rather than writing follow-up tasks from a meeting in your notebook, record them on your to-do list or send yourself an email summarizing them. If you have multiple voicemail boxes, see if it's possible to forward your school phone to your personal voicemail. If colleagues make requests of you via text message, you might ask them to send such requests by email instead. The fewer inboxes you manage, the easier it'll be to get current so you can feel good about getting into classrooms.

Regardless of the specific tools you use, strive to minimize the number of inboxes containing action items by routing tasks into a few central locations.

Reduce Interruptions From Non-Emergency Communication

When a communication medium—such as a two-way radio—doesn't have an inbox, the only way to stay current with it is to allow yourself to be interrupted every time a request comes in and either handle the request immediately or transfer it into another system, such as a sticky note or your electronic to-do list, where you can keep track of it over time. While it may be necessary to allow certain emergency situations to interrupt you at any time, most of your communication and coordination with other staff should happen through non-interrupting communication media that have reliable inboxes you can check and process on your own schedule.

If your staff has adopted the habit of sending you text messages about non-urgent matters, or if your office staff has developed a habit of reaching you via two-way radio for non-emergency communications, it may be time to reset expectations so you can protect your time in classrooms. Simply ask that they send you an email, note, or voicemail, and make sure you follow up when they do. If your colleagues know you'll get back to them, they'll be more willing to simply leave you a message, and less likely to resort to interrupting forms of communication.

Avoid "Fuzzy" Channels for Important Requests

As social media networks grow in popularity, the *feed* or *stream* has become a popular alternative to the inbox, and often the quantity of information arriving in this format is quite vast and difficult to keep up with. For example, schools that use Slack or group text messages instead of two-way radios may find these smartphone-based messaging platforms easier to use, but they lack a critical feature: the inbox. Similarly, the number of apps that send messages in their own unique format, such as Voxer, Twitter, and Facebook Messenger, has grown. These stream-based communication channels are more fuzzy than inbox-oriented media such as email.

In a stream, older messages are constantly pushed farther down by newer messages, yet they cannot be organized, marked as unread, moved to folders, transformed into tasks or calendar appointments, or forwarded.

Notifications such as app alerts can help you notice what's relevant to you personally, but don't help you keep track of it over time. Text messages, chat, and other push notifications may facilitate immediate communication but don't lend themselves to thorough follow-up; it's too easy to lose track of action items in the midst of a high volume of nonactionable communication. If you notice that your colleagues are using these formats to communicate with you, it may be necessary to insist that they make these requests through email or another nonstream medium, routing them to a reliable inbox so you don't miss anything important.

Once you've eliminated fuzzy inputs and minimized disruptive channels of communication, you can focus on developing a consistent method for processing your inboxes. You can use the same method for email, voicemail, paper mail, tasks, and any other inbox-based medium.

Process Your Inboxes

Before you start organizing and scheduling your work, eliminate as much as possible through brutally honest *triage*. Not every task that lands in one of your inboxes is going to get done—that's just the reality. Rather than overcommit and plan unrealistically, decide up front what is worthy of your scarce time and attention, and communicate clearly and honestly with everyone who makes requests of you.

Process your inboxes one at a time, in the order that makes the most sense to you. For example, transcribe and delete voicemail messages first, so you're not distracted by the unknowns they hold. You may want to process your email inbox last, since clearing other inboxes may generate new emails—for example, if you deal with a handwritten note by taking a photo with your phone and emailing it to yourself.

As you process each inbox, keep in mind that it's not enough to review everything and process *most* of it; it's best to process every item, without exception, until that inbox is completely empty. Only when you have reviewed and made a decision about *every* item in your inbox can you claim to be current—and only then can you step away from your desk and visit classrooms without being distracted by all of your unfinished work. Empty your key inboxes every day—perhaps several times a day for some, such as voicemail, that contain more urgent items.

Only when you have reviewed and made a decision about every item in your inbox can you claim to be current—and only then can you step away from your desk and visit classrooms without being distracted by all of your unfinished work.

If you don't completely empty an inbox, you'll start to develop a backlog of unprocessed tasks that will make you less and less able to plan your day realistically. This may not matter at first, if just a few items are left unresolved, but when your backlog has grown to dozens of items, you can no longer evaluate, triage, and plan your work for the day. Every item must be either deleted, completed, delegated, or deferred; simply make the decision to take one of these four actions with each item (Allen, 2015).

Work your way through each inbox, from top to bottom. For voicemail, simply write messages down in the order they play, and delete them immediately. For email, process newer messages first, because older messages may already be outdated due to more recent replies. You may want to enable discussion threading, in which all replies to one message are grouped together, if it's not already turned on by default in your email program. For hard copy items, open envelopes, turn multi-page documents to the relevant page, and use sticky notes to highlight action items.

If you encounter items you can handle immediately—in, say, two minutes or less—take care of them as you're processing the inbox. For example, you can unsubscribe from an unwanted email newsletter in just a few seconds, then delete the email and move on. If you need to delegate a task, do so immediately, while you're processing your inbox. Defer the rest for later. (The tasks you defer will be discussed in more detail in chapter 8, page 69.)

There's always a tradeoff between getting through your inbox more quickly versus creating additional work by postponing things that you could do immediately. For most people the *two-minute rule* is a help-ful guide: if you can finish a task in under two minutes and never have to worry about it again, do it immediately. If it'll take longer than two minutes, postpone it for a time when you're not trying to empty your inbox (Allen, 2015). If you're deferring a task that has arrived via email, you may want to either transfer it to your electronic task app or take advantage of your email app's built-in scheduling functionality. Kevin Kruse (2015) argues that scheduling tasks on a calendar results in more effective follow-through and more realistic planning than using a to-do list. Fortunately, most email programs allow users to turn messages into tasks or calendar appointments with just a few clicks.

Following the delete, complete, delegate, and defer process will allow you to feel enormously satisfied when emptying your inboxes. This habit is essential for getting into classrooms every day. You'll gain incredible peace of mind from knowing that you aren't leaving a chaotic mess behind every time you step into the hall and head to a classroom. Instead of feeling that you need to be in the office so you don't miss something important, you can be confident that your inboxes will do what they've been designed to do—collect and store new inputs until you process them (Allen, 2015). When you return, you can process each inbox so you stay current on your most urgent work.

Day 7 Action Challenge: Streamline Your Inboxes and Communication

Make a list of all the communication channels and inboxes that currently bring you important action items. For example, you may want to reflect on the following questions.

- ‣ Do staff routinely text me with important requests?
- ‣ Does my school use an intranet, a chat app, or a learning management system for important communication?
- ‣ Do I keep notes on paper in my pocket or in composition notebooks?

Identify all of the channels containing action items, and look for ways to route them into reliable inboxes. Reduce interrupting channels, and ask your staff not to send you action items via fuzzy channels such as social media.

Remember to have a brief conversation with the teacher after each classroom visit, and strive to finish your first cycle in the next week and a half.

8

Managing the Work
You're Not Doing Yet

Visiting classrooms on a regular basis means leaving certain other work unfinished. You must organize everything that you don't handle immediately into a reliable system that you can easily use to make decisions about how to spend your time. Most instructional leaders don't have a single system, though—it's far more common to have tasks scattered across multiple tools, media, and physical locations. As a result, it's very difficult for most instructional leaders to maintain a clear sense of what they could be working on so they can prioritize what they *should* be working on. If emails hold some of your unfinished work, while stacks of paper contain other priorities, and yet still other to-dos are sitting in notebooks and on legal pads, you'll find it very difficult to comprehend the big picture and choose what to work on each day—and, just as critically, what *not* to work on.

Most people conceive of their to-do list as a set of tasks that they should do immediately, but the most important use of a to-do list is to organize the work you're *not* doing yet. The reason for this distinction is simple: if, throughout the day, you're constantly checking your to-do list for what to work on next, you're constantly making decisions—decisions that you should instead make in advance. And if your to-do list has more than a dozen or so items, it becomes unwieldy to repeatedly review and prioritize. Thus, in this chapter, you'll learn to manage the work you're not doing yet by separating planning from doing; using a task-management app; keeping your task lists short; and prioritizing strengths, weaknesses, opportunities, and threats.

Separate Planning From Doing

It's essential to separate *planning your work* from *doing your work* because you're far more likely to make sound prioritization and scheduling decisions when you aren't faced with doing the work immediately. To understand why, consider a time-consuming and unpleasant task, such as writing a detailed status report for a grant. If you plan to work on this task tomorrow, you can set aside time on your calendar; the unpleasantness of actually doing the work is far enough off that it doesn't stop you from making the right decision. If you don't plan your work in advance and simply start the day hoping you get around to the report, everything else you could be doing instead will compete with the report for your time and attention throughout the day. Unfortunately, most of this other work is likely to be easier than the taxing and time-consuming process of writing the report. When you've decided what to work on in advance, you don't have to decide what to work on moment by moment; you simply follow your plan, and you can devote your full attention to the work itself rather than the process of reprioritizing. The more we can eliminate unnecessary decision making throughout the day, the more we'll sustain the energy we need to do our best work.

The more we can eliminate unnecessary decision making throughout the day, the more we'll sustain the energy we need to do our best work.

Use a Task-Management App

In order to plan your day realistically and ensure that you achieve your most important goals, it's essential to process the wide range of inputs—the sources of information about what you could, should, or must work on—and consolidate them in a single, centralized location. You may find that email is the closest thing you have to a single, centralized system, but your email inbox is poorly suited to keep track of the prioritization and organization decisions you'll need to make. Sorting messages by date, sender, or subject isn't enough; you need the full power of an electronic task-management app, such as Todoist (available at www.todoist.com), to make optimal decisions about how to spend your time.

From start to finish, an electronic task-management app allows you to easily do the following.

- Capture inputs from email and other sources, as well as verbal requests, by quickly creating new tasks in the app's inbox.
- Triage and process your *task* inbox after processing other inboxes such as voicemail and email.
- Organize tasks into specific lists to prioritize, plan, and schedule your work using your calendar, meeting agendas, and other tools.

Your task-management app can provide a single *mission control* dashboard where you can make all of your prioritization and time-management decisions in advance so your days are filled with action, not paralyzing decisions over what to work on next.

If you don't have a robust task-management app, I recommend Todoist, because it's simple to learn, has a free version as well as a premium one with enhanced features, and has apps for virtually every device and operating system.

Capture Inputs From Other Inboxes

Your electronic task-management app should contain an *inbox* area so you can quickly add new tasks throughout the day as they occur to you. The inbox feature is present in most dedicated task apps, and its function is to allow you to distinguish tasks that you haven't yet processed from those you've already organized into more specific lists. For example, as you listen to your voicemails, you may want to add tasks directly in your task app's inbox, so you can be sure to follow up on each message. When a teacher stops you in the hall to make a request, you can quickly note this task in your inbox, where you'll be sure to take care of it later. You can even dictate the task by using your smartphone or tablet's voice-to-text transcription feature.

Some cloud-based task-management apps also have the ability to receive tasks via email (and potentially via other means such as your smartphone's voice assistant) so you can add tasks to your inbox without even opening the app. This frees you from having to organize tasks into specific lists at the time you record them, which may take up more time than you can spare. It's essential to be able to record a new idea quickly and get back to what you were doing; if the process is cumbersome, you'll revert to using sticky notes or other systems that don't give you a single, consolidated list of everything on your plate.

It's essential to be able to record a new idea quickly and get back to what you were doing.

Triage and Process Your Task Inbox

It's important to process and clear all of your inboxes daily, and your task app's inbox is no exception. You may want to clear your task inbox several times throughout the day to ensure that you deal with time-sensitive matters—such as calling parents about discipline issues—before it's too late. The first step is triage—quickly identifying issues that need to be handled immediately—while also culling tasks that have already been completed or are no longer important. As with clearing your email inbox, you may want to follow a two-minute rule to quickly deal with small tasks.

Then, process the remaining tasks by organizing them into more specific lists or scheduling them on your calendar. In order to plan the next day effectively, it's essential to get a clear overview of everything you need to accomplish, and your task app is the perfect place to gain this overview.

Organize Tasks and Schedule Work

While you may be accustomed to using a daily to-do list to ensure that you finish everything essential by the end of the day, a task-management app's main contribution to your productivity is as a planning tool, not as a checklist to guide you throughout the day. More than a simple to-do list, a task-management app allows you to quickly record tasks, organize these tasks into lists, and set additional fields such as due date, priority, required time, required energy, and other properties that will help you organize your work and decide how to spend your time. You can then schedule these tasks on your calendar, which will force you to realistically allocate time to the work that most deserves it.

Other tasks may fit into recurring meetings that are already on your calendar, such as staff meetings, leadership committee meetings, and check-ins with your supervisor, office staff, and admin team. Create a list in your task-management app for each of these recurring meetings, and treat it as a draft agenda for upcoming meetings. Whenever you encounter an issue that would best be handled in one of these settings, put it on the appropriate agenda list. Then, when it's time to prepare the formal agenda for an upcoming meeting, review its agenda list in your task-management app, and identify the most important issues to address in the meeting. Or, if there's no need to prepare a formal agenda, simply review the list when you're about to meet with the corresponding person or group.

If you use other tools, such as email reminders or shared documents, to coordinate and prepare for upcoming meetings, you can simply copy items from the appropriate list in your task-management app. This is yet another advantage of having a single, consolidated electronic system to manage your unfinished work.

You may find that once you're using your task-management app successfully, it becomes easier to process your email, because you no longer need to use email as a task-management tool. However, don't rush into converting all of your old emails into tasks. It's best to wait until you've developed a reliable habit of using your task app to manage and plan your work; if you turn all of your emails into tasks right away, it's likely to become overwhelming, and you may be tempted to abandon the task app entirely. Instead, ease into it: record new tasks in your task app, continue to handle tasks that will take less than two minutes while you process your email inbox, and schedule critical time-consuming tasks on your calendar or on the appropriate meeting agenda.

Keep Your Task Lists Short

As an instructional leader, you face constant choices about what to work on. There's always more to do than you can possibly accomplish, so you must select the tasks you'll *actually* work on from a much larger set of tasks you *could* work on.

In his book *The Paradox of Choice: Why More Is Less*, psychologist Barry Schwartz (2004) explains the downside of having too many choices: our brains become overwhelmed with all the possibilities and search for ways to simplify the decision. A good rule of thumb is that ten options is the most we can handle; any more than ten, and we stop deciding rationally and start deciding using what psychologists who study decision making call *substitution*. When we fall prey to substitution, we may think we're making a rational decision to work on the task that's the best use of our time, but in fact we've swapped in other criteria—such as convenience or novelty—to simplify the decision. If you have twenty-five tasks on your list, you're likely to choose one to work on based on, say, how enjoyable or easy it is, rather than on how important it is.

Over time, substitution can cause you to spend a great deal of your time completing tasks that ultimately have very little impact on student learning. While it may feel good to check off tasks as you quickly complete them, it's unwise to always prioritize the easiest tasks. Instead, exercise self-discipline to plan ahead and make careful, thoughtful decisions about what matters most.

These prioritization decisions get easier to make when you're considering fewer options, so it helps to organize your tasks into shorter lists within your task-management app. To keep your lists short, you can filter tasks by due date, energy level required, and other criteria that you find helpful. Modern task-management apps, such as Todoist, allow you to create multiple views for different purposes, so it's easy to whittle down a long list into only the most relevant tasks.

Prioritize Strengths, Weaknesses, Opportunities, and Threats

As you review the many tasks in your task-management app, how can you make better decisions about how to allocate your limited time to what matters most? The U.S. military uses the acronym SWOT— *strengths, weaknesses, opportunities,* and *threats*—to prioritize among possible courses of action (Bensoussan & Fleisher, 2013). In your leadership role, you can do the same by asking yourself questions such as the following.

- "What actions should I take to build on my *strengths* so I can have the greatest possible impact?"
- "What *weaknesses* in our school or in my leadership need the most immediate attention?"
- "What are our biggest current *opportunities* for improvement?"
- "What external forces or internal dynamics could pose *threats* to our school community and our work?"

You'll notice that these questions go beyond the usual criteria we use to make decisions as educators, such as whether a practice is evidence based, whether a decision is data-driven, or whether the majority of staff support it. Even if we limited ourselves only to options that are research-based, data-driven, and popular with teachers, we'd have far too many potential areas of focus. The possibilities for what we could be spending our time on are endless.

The first act of leadership is to decide what matters. Starting with your school's mission, vision, and goals, you can use the SWOT framework to filter tasks from your task-management app before they make it to your calendar. Another way to frame this filtering process is by examining the potential consequences of working on (or choosing not to work on) certain tasks. As you review your lists, ask yourself, "What are the implications of working on this task *vis-à-vis* our current strengths, weaknesses, opportunities, and threats? What are the implications of not working on it?" You may find that this makes it easier to clarify your highest and most immediate priorities.

The first act of leadership is to decide what matters.

Using a task-management app can be intimidating, because you have so many tasks to consider. We naturally tend to avoid long, daunting lists of tasks, or keep separate systems—like sticky notes on our desks—that allow us to narrow our focus. However comforting it may be to have some important tasks hidden away in a notebook, or saved in an email that you've repeatedly marked as unread, we make the best decisions about how to spend our time when we have all of the relevant information in one place. If you're currently storing tasks in different locations, now is the time to create a *mission control* dashboard for your work by starting to use a task-management app.

Day 8 Action Challenge: Link Everything to Your Task-Management App's Inbox

Review the results of your Action Challenge from chapter 7 (Streamline Your Inboxes and Communication, page 67), and identify ways to get all of your important reminders into your task inbox. For example, you may find that you can forward tasks residing in your email inbox to a special email address that your task-management app provides.

For anything that technology can't automate for you, identify the steps you'll need to take to route potential tasks into the app. For example, you may want to develop the habit of transferring tasks from meeting notes that you take in your paper notebook throughout the day into your task-management app at the end of the day. As potential distractions arise throughout the school day, jot them in your task app's inbox so you can stay focused on your goal of visiting three classrooms per day.

You may want to consider the following questions for reflection.

‣ What systems for keeping track of tasks have I tried but abandoned in the past?

‣ What communication channels do other people use to make requests of me? Which of these am I most likely to overlook?

‣ What kinds of tasks do I tend to leave unfinished the longest?

9

Organizing Your To-Do List

As we discussed in chapter 8 (page 69), we experience cognitive overload when we face choosing among more than about ten items. Since you always have far more tasks or projects you could be working on, it's essential to create a system that allows you to narrow your focus, no matter how busy you may become. In this chapter, we'll explore ways you can organize your task-management app to prevent it from becoming overwhelming so it's always your go-to dashboard for planning your day.

The key to creating a manageable system is to use multiple well-organized lists within your app, rather than a single large list, and to set additional properties for each task—such as priority or due date—that will allow you to filter out tasks according to criteria you set. With modern task-management apps such as Todoist, this is quick and easy, and we'll consider several approaches: organizing by action with the PEEP approach; and organizing by due date, time required, and energy level.

Organize by Action With the PEEP Approach

As you process your task inbox, you may find patterns of items that you can naturally group together and process in batches. For example, you may be in the habit of writing your staff newsletter on Sunday evenings, or you may prepare the agenda for your weekly leadership team meetings on Tuesday mornings. When you find items that belong in these groups, create a *bucket*—a separate list—for them in your task-management app. In Todoist, these lists are called *projects*, but they may also be called *folders* or *lists* depending on the app you're using. As you process your task inbox, route each item to the appropriate list. Then, when it's time to batch-process those items—for example, by writing the news-letter or preparing the agenda—simply review the list, deal with each item, and you'll be confident that you haven't missed anything. If time constraints prevent you from including every item—especially for meeting agendas—having a single list will allow you to quickly prioritize the most important items.

By separating specific batchable groups from your more miscellaneous lists, you can both increase your productivity in your batched work and keep your miscellaneous lists from growing too long. It's essentially the same approach you'd use to organize your home—if you want to clean a cluttered room, you can't toss everything in the junk drawer; you need to put everything away where it belongs, and that requires that you have specific storage locations for most of the items you're putting away. There will still be a few things that go in the junk drawer, but most items should have a specific place where they belong. I call this approach *PEEP—a place for everything and everything in its place.*

By separating specific batchable groups from your more miscellaneous lists, you can both increase your productivity in your batched work and keep your miscellaneous lists from growing too long.

PEEP saves time and effort by reducing the amount of decision making necessary for processing your inboxes and batch-processing your work. When a batchable item arrives in your inbox, and you already have a bucket for that type of item, it's easy to process it—but only if you organize your tasks according to the *action* you need to take, not according to abstract categories or areas of responsibility. For example, you may have numerous tasks related to instructional leadership, but since the manner in which you'll handle these tasks varies widely, it would not be helpful to create an *instructional leadership* bucket; a list of tasks conceptually related to instructional leadership isn't any easier to manage than a list of miscellaneous tasks. In daily life, we organize according to the actions we need to take, rather than by conceptual category. Think about your shoes, for example—you wouldn't keep them in your sock drawer just because they're conceptually related to feet; they belong on the floor, because that's where you take them off and put them on. This is an important distinction: PEEP helps you organize your tasks by action, not by category.

PEEP can also help you organize groups of tasks that aren't batchable, but instead need to be done in a specific order. Many projects fall into this category; for example, if you're applying for a grant, you may need to complete a number of steps, such as reviewing the grant application, getting input from teachers, drafting a budget, and so forth, in a particular order. While other tasks may be conceptually related to the grant—for example, informing your PTA—if they aren't sequential steps, it's not helpful to include them in the list. You can instead include these tasks on more miscellaneous lists, or on other lists such as meeting agendas. When you're working sequentially through a project, if you encounter a task that isn't the next necessary action, you'll have to stop and re-prioritize, defeating the purpose of having a well-organized list. Remember, you don't want to have to constantly reorganize your to-do list throughout the day and choose what to work on; it's best to separate deciding from doing. When you've already made decisions about what to work on, you can simply review your lists and calendar and get to work.

Organize by Due Date, Time Required, and Energy Level

After you've optimized your buckets to organize all of your batchable work into specific lists and created separate lists for sequential projects, you may still find that you have long, unmanageable lists of miscellaneous tasks that you need to complete. When these lists become too long, we start to avoid them—defeating the purpose of using a task-management app. Your app can help you apply additional criteria to filter out tasks that you can't or shouldn't do immediately. Modern apps such as Todoist have a search feature that allows you to set specific criteria for the tasks you want to see, and you can save these searches as filters. For example, you could do a search for tasks that have the priority field set to *high* and the due date field set to *today*. If you accomplish all of your high-priority tasks, you can use a different search or filter to view tasks that are due *today* and have a priority of *medium*.

Modern task-management apps have numerous fields, or properties, that can be set to help you plan your work. You won't need to use all of these fields for every task; doing so would make the process of adding a task to the app too cumbersome. In fact, you may not want to set any of these fields when adding new tasks—an important function of the task inbox is to allow you to add items quickly, without filling in the additional fields. You can then update these fields when you're process- ing your task inbox.

You can use your own combinations of these fields to make precise decisions about what to focus on. First, you may find it helpful to use the *priority* field when you're reviewing your lists and picking out the most important tasks, but the reality is that many tasks will be high priority. A long list full of high-priority tasks is no more manageable than a list of unprioritized tasks. For many people, *due date* is an essential filter.

A long list full of high-priority tasks is no more manageable than a list of unprioritized tasks.

It may be tempting to set a due date of *today* for nearly all tasks, and by itself, this isn't a problem. You may choose to use *due today* to mean *review today*. You must ensure, though, that you don't leave any *due today* tasks unfinished and unreviewed. If you aren't going to get to something today, don't let it become overdue, or you'll no longer have a system you can trust. Instead, change the due date, or admit that you're never going to do it and mark it off your list. By the end of the day, empty your task inbox, and either do or deliberately postpone every task marked as *due today* in your task-management app.

Other fields are also useful in certain situations. For more random and one-off tasks, you may want to add properties such as *time required*, *context*, and *energy level*, because this will help you decide how to allo- cate your time. If your task-management app doesn't have all of these fields, you can use the *tag* or *label* field to create your own scheme. For example, you might use the *label* field in Todoist to identify tasks you can do in less than ten minutes with the label "10 min." Being able to filter your tasks by the amount of time they'll require can help you squeeze more into the odd blocks of time you find yourself with throughout the day—when you might otherwise check email aimlessly. If you have ten minutes to work at your desk, and you have a filter set for miscellaneous tasks you can complete in ten minutes, you'll be far more productive than if you have to review long lists of tasks that don't have this property set.

Another way to filter tasks is by context. *Context* specifies the setting or location in which you'll perform a task, or the tools or information you'll need to have with you (Allen, 2015). As our smartphones and other mobile devices become more powerful, context is becoming less relevant than it once was, but there are still many types of work that you must do in a specific location. Some task-management apps can even remind you when you arrive at a specific location that you've linked to certain tasks; if so, take advantage of this feature to avoid making a separate trip later—for example, you may have several tasks on your list at any given time that can only be done at district headquarters. If you set a location-based reminder for each of these tasks, your app can remind you to complete all of them when you arrive. If your app doesn't have this feature, you can simply check your "district headquarters" filter manually when you arrive at the district office.

You might also find it helpful to use the *context* field to identify tasks that involve a specific person, such as a team leader, your supervisor, or your administrative assistant. Since these tasks may be scattered across multiple lists within your task app, it's useful to be able to search for all tasks involving a certain person when you're about to talk with that person. As you make your way around campus for classroom visits and other duties, you can accomplish these tasks quickly, without having to make separate trips or phone calls.

Lastly, if you want to maximize your productivity, planning around your natural variations in mental energy is essential. You may be at your best when you first arrive at school, before students and colleagues are around. Or you may hit your stride midmorning, when you can reach everyone you need to work with. If you save your most cognitively demanding work for times in the day when you aren't at your best, you may find that you tend to procrastinate or do an inferior job. Conversely, if you schedule busywork (such as tidying up your office) during your peak productivity time, you may become anxious and frustrated that you aren't accomplishing something more challenging. In your task app, you may find it helpful to mark tasks as *low energy* or *high energy* or even *doable while watching TV*. Identify the different energy levels you experience throughout the day, and match your miscellaneous tasks to the optimal time. Then, use filters to find tasks that match your energy level, and get to work.

Out of Sight, Out of Mind, but Not Out of Control

When you develop an effective system for keeping track of your work, you gain a new freedom: the freedom to put the work you aren't doing yet out of sight and out of mind, with confidence that you'll return to it later and follow up when the time is right. You can then spend more time visiting classrooms without the burden of doubt and fear that you're overlooking something crucial.

If you don't have such a system, clutter is inevitable, because it serves as a tangible reminder of your unfinished work. Yet this clutter comes with a cost—a cost we can avoid by effectively tracking our unfinished work using an electronic task-management app, and organizing it using the strategies in this chapter.

Day 9 Action Challenge: Set Up Your PEEPs

In your electronic task-management app, create at least five permanent buckets that you can use to hold tasks that you can batch-process, such as announcements to mention in your parent newsletter, agenda items for your leadership team, and so on. Next, set up as many project-specific buckets as you need. Be sure to break down your large, miscellaneous lists into action-oriented lists rather than conceptual categories. For miscellaneous items, set fields such as due date and context to make it easier to identify the most relevant tasks with filters.

As you continue your visits to approximately three classrooms each day, and as you make your way around campus, use the *context* field to find tasks related to the people you encounter, so you can check off multiple items at once.

You may want to consider the following questions for reflection.

- Whom did I speak with today that should have a dedicated *agenda* bucket in my task-management app, so I can easily track any items I'll need to speak with him or her about?

- What major sequential projects am I currently working on?

- What's a conceptual category I've been using to organize my tasks? How could I convert this into an action-based organization scheme instead?

10

Maximizing Your Mental Energy With Habits

How can you make daily visits to classrooms not just an occasional activity but a consistent habit? As with any project, it starts with budgeting key resources. As an instructional leader, your most valuable resources are time and mental energy. It's critical to ensure that you're allocating enough time and mental energy to your practice of visiting classrooms, but often these resources are sapped by the other demands of your role. As we'll explore in this chapter, research has uncovered a surprising link between habits and mental energy that can help you harness the mental energy you need to make it into classrooms daily. In this chapter, we will learn how patterns become habits, understand how habits work, see why habits matter, learn how to conserve mental energy with habits, and discover five ways to change habits.

Learn How Patterns Become Habits

As we've discussed in the last few chapters, preplanning how you'll spend your time is essential for prioritizing your work effectively, which makes it far easier to get into classrooms. You'll never get into classrooms if you wait until there's nothing else to do; you'll *always* have unfinished tasks that compete with the work of visiting classrooms and talking with teachers. If you don't plan ahead, and instead decide moment by moment what most deserves your time and attention, you'll naturally gravitate to low-priority, high-urgency tasks. Planning your day ahead of time by using your task-management app and calendar saves you from making decisions throughout the day about what matters at any given moment. As you engage in this planning process, day after day, you'll start to realize what works for you and what tends not to work. In large part, these patterns reflect your habits. The better your habits, the more productive you'll be.

The better your habits, the more productive you'll be.

Researchers estimate that more than 40 percent of what we do in any given day is driven by habits (Duhigg, 2012). From brushing your teeth to driving to work to microwaving your lunch, habits govern most of the predictable aspects of your day. Habits also govern many of your responses to situations that arise unpredictably throughout the day, such as staff members asking, "Got a minute?" Yet most of the time, we form habits accidentally rather than intentionally. We fall into patterns based on what we do the first time we encounter a situation, or what we've seen others do. We thus stumble into most of the decisions that govern nearly half of our lives.

What's more, the demands that school leaders face condition us to be reactive (Mintzberg, 1973). Others expect us to respond as needs arise, even if it means disrupting our plans. We become accustomed to interruptions, so we learn to be flexible and adaptable. Yet we still rely heavily on habits—just not habits we've chosen on purpose.

Understand How Habits Work

According to Pulitzer Prize–winning journalist Charles Duhigg (2012), author of *The Power of Habit*, there are three essential components to any habit. First is the *cue*, the stimulus that triggers a near-automatic response. Just about anything can serve as a cue; cues can be internal or external; tangible and obvious; or subtle and invisible. Common types of cues include chronological cues, such as the time of day or elapsed time; emotions, such as anger or happiness; physical sensations, such as hunger or fatigue; environmental cues, such as temperature and lighting; tool-based cues, such as alarms and reminders; interpersonal cues, such as facial expressions, tone, or words; criterion-based cues, such as standards, checklists, or rubrics; and instrument-based cues, like the reading on a speedometer or gas gauge. As you can see, we can manage some of these cues, but others simply occur outside of our control.

The second part of the habit loop is the *sequence*, which is our response to the cue. When your alarm clock goes off (cue), you may respond by hitting the snooze button (sequence). Since many cues are unavoidable, the sequence is our clearest opportunity to modify our habits. For example, if you want to stop hitting the snooze button, you can turn your alarm off the first time it goes off and start getting ready for the day.

The third phase of the habit loop is the *reward*, which creates a powerful sense of anticipation that drives your behavioral response to the cue. Hitting the snooze button gives you the reward of a few more minutes of sleep. Eating a snack gives you the reward of feeling satisfied instead of hungry. Because your brain has been conditioned to anticipate the reward, you start to experience the pleasure of the reward before you've even earned it—and this pleasure compels you to carry out the sequence, even if the sequence itself is difficult or unpleasant. Understanding this three-part cycle—cue, sequence, reward—and the anticipation mechanism that ties it together allows us to modify our habits to increase our effectiveness. (For a further discussion on ways to modify habits, see Discover Five Ways to Change Habits, page 91.)

As you consider these strategies, think about the habits you currently employ to get through the day, and identify habits that you may need to modify or replace in order to get into classrooms every day.

See Why Habits Matter

Habits carry us through much of the day by occurring on autopilot, so we can conserve our mental energy for the aspects of our work that need it most. Throughout the day, we encounter many situations that demand our mental energy, such as thinking critically about what we see in a classroom observation, triaging problems as they arise, and dealing with emotionally challenging situations (Baumeister & Tierney, 2011). We handle some of these situations *ad hoc*—that is, by making decisions as they arise—and some by habit.

> *Habits carry us through much of the day by occuring on autopilot, so we can conserve our mental energy for the aspects of our work that need it most.*

Because they're deeply ingrained, habits require less cognitive effort to carry out successfully; as athletes well know, practice leads to *automaticity*. This automaticity has several sources. One is the muscle memory that we develop as we master any physical task, such as throwing a baseball or driving a car. Our brains still tell our muscles what to do, but with so little conscious thought that it truly feels automatic. Automaticity also comes from learned routines that we mentally chunk together to reduce their cognitive load. If you make coffee at home every morning, you've likely become accustomed to your particular coffee maker and can brew a pot without even thinking about all the steps—changing the filter, measuring the grounds, adding water, and so on. You know exactly how to operate your coffee maker, and you know exactly where everything is. But when you're away from home, using an unfamiliar coffee maker, everything is harder. You must search for the coffee and filters, and you must devote extra attention to figuring out how to operate the coffee maker. If you've ever noticed how the most basic daily routines seem to take longer when you're on vacation—and leave you feeling surprisingly tired—you've experienced what researchers call *ego depletion* (Baumeister & Tierney, 2011).

In their book *Willpower: Rediscovering the Greatest Human Strength*, researcher Roy F. Baumeister and journalist John Tierney (2011) explain that what we call *mental energy* is in fact a measurable and finite capacity, which they term *willpower*. As this energy wanes throughout the day, we enter a state of *ego depletion*, when we have exhausted our mental energy and our willpower drops precipitously. In our ego-depleted state, we don't feel like doing challenging work, just as you might feel late at night—but ego depletion is different from physical exhaustion. It can occur at any time of day, based on a number of factors.

Baumeister's research has found, through a series of brilliant experiments, that rest, glucose, and other factors have a positive impact on our willpower (Baumeister & Tierney, 2011). As you might expect, being tired or hungry tends to reduce your willpower, but there are other, more surprising factors too, and these factors are relevant for our work as instructional leaders.

First, *emotional self-regulation* is a major contributor to ego depletion. If you're in a verbal confrontation with a parent or student, keeping your cool is the way to keep your job, but it will take a toll on your mental energy for the day. Letting your emotions show may result in less ego depletion, but the consequences are usually not worth the cost.

Second, and perhaps more surprising, is Baumeister's finding that *repeated decision making* is a major contributor to ego depletion—even if the decisions are exceedingly minor (Baumeister & Tierney, 2011). Tasks as simple as filing papers and emails into folders can rapidly deplete your mental energy because they require so many small decisions. But there's a workaround: *habits* don't involve actively making a decision in the moment—since you have already made the decision and turned it into an automatic response—so anything we do by habit will exact very little cost in terms of mental energy.

These nuances of the research on ego depletion may not be widely understood in our society, but it's easy to identify practical examples. The late Steve Jobs of Apple, who sported his famous black turtlenecks at nearly every public appearance, wasn't just making a fashion statement— he was eliminating a decision (what to wear) from his schedule each morning, so he could devote more of his mental energy to running a multibillion-dollar company. Another example is the familiar experience of feeling overwhelmed in a new job. New teachers, for example, may feel overwhelmed by the sheer number of decisions they must make, and total exhaustion is the norm at the end of the day. Over time, these decisions become habitual responses, and the job becomes somewhat less exhausting as teachers gain experience. When there's a new curriculum, a new group of students, or a change in the schedule, though, the added cognitive burden of additional decision making takes a toll on willpower.

Knowing what affects our willpower, and knowing that habits are a workaround for conserving willpower, how can we purposefully deploy habits to maximize our effectiveness? In the following section, we'll explore several strategies for modifying your day so you can devote your mental energy to your most important work.

Conserve Mental Energy With Habits

If we want to both conserve energy for what matters most and ensure that we're highly effective in everything we do, we can't merely continue to follow the habits we've developed by default; we must design and construct the habits we need. If you've wondered how you can find the mental energy to get into classrooms on a daily basis, in addition to the work that's already pushing you to your limits, habits are the answer. What changes might we make to optimize our habits?

First, the simplest and highest-impact habit change you can make immediately is to shift low-level decision making to the end of the day. Scheduling, processing non-urgent emails, and updating your task-management app can all wait until the end of the day, after you've completed your most cognitively demanding work—such as visiting classrooms and talking with teachers. The work itself may be cognitively demanding, but merely processing messages and to-do items in your inboxes isn't as demanding. Remember, if you separate *deciding* from *doing*, you'll make better, faster decisions, and you'll be more focused and less fatigued while you're actually doing the work. This habit has two key components: (1) deciding *not* to do low-level decision making at your peak times in the day and (2) deciding when you'll do it instead. You may elect to process email and tasks right before you leave for the day, or you may prefer to catch up later in the evening before bed.

Remember, if you separate deciding from doing, you'll make better, faster decisions, and you'll be more focused and less fatigued while you're actually doing the work.

Whatever you do, shift the bulk of this high-volume, low-cognition decision making out of your morning, so it's not triggering ego depletion too early in the day.

The second way to leverage habits is to create rewarding benchmarks, or daily goals, for yourself. If you commit to emptying your email inbox every evening and emptying your voicemail before lunch each day, sticking to these habits will start to provide mental rewards—your brain will experience a rush of dopamine each time your inbox reads "0 messages," and this will reinforce the habit (Duhigg, 2012). Similarly, when you establish a daily goal of three classroom visits, you'll experience a mental reward when you reach your goal. These small rewards can help offset the natural tendency to avoid challenging work and can create a sense of productive momentum that carries you through the day. Now that we have an idea of how habits function and how they can help us optimize our use of mental energy, we'll look at five ways we can shape our habits.

Discover Five Ways to Change Habits

The first and most direct way to change your habits is to *replace the sequence*. All you need is a personal rule that you can apply whenever the situation arises. For example, *If I feel hungry, I'll eat a fiber bar instead of a cookie*. So, if you're hungry (cue), instead of a cookie, eat a fiber bar (sequence), and you'll still feel satisfied (reward). If this substitution actually works, it can be easy to change a habit (Duhigg, 2012). For example, if you find that you're wasting time at your desk in the afternoons instead of getting into classrooms, you can identify the cue (time of day), reward (feeling accomplished), and the sequence you want to change (doing office work). Then, simply replace the sequence with a better alternative—getting into classrooms. Too often, though, the new sequence doesn't result in quite the same reward. If your healthy snack isn't as tasty as the cookies you're used to, it'll be hard to break your cookie habit. If you enjoy the mental break you get from doing busy-work in the office, it'll be hard to develop a habit of visiting classrooms in the afternoon instead. In other words, if the sequence doesn't trigger the same rewards, it won't create a sense of anticipation next time the cue arises, and it'll have no habit-forming power at all. So, we need a few more strategies to optimize our habits.

The second way to modify your habits is to *disrupt the routine*. This works especially well for habits with ever-present cues but weak rewards. For example, if you find that you get drawn into answering email or doing other work at your desk every time you stop by the office, instead of getting into classrooms, you can make it impractical to sit at your desk by, say, having your administrative assistant put a sign marked *Classrooms* on your chair every time you have class visits scheduled on your calendar. When you see the sign, your habitual response of sitting down and doing some office work will be disrupted, and you can start to form a new habit of obeying your calendar.

The third way to change habits is to *alter the reward equation*. What if you have an unhelpful habit, such as leaving your cluttered desk and inbox for tomorrow, that gives you a short-term reward? If you get to go home without thinking about the mess you're leaving behind, you're obtaining a mental reward that you will need to offset somehow. You might obtain a natural reward from getting everything cleaned up and organized for the next day, but this may be less tempting than the easier route of leaving the mess for tomorrow. You can alter this balance by tying a negative consequence to the undesirable routine—for example, you could leave a twenty-dollar bill pinned to your bulletin board, and let your custodian know to take it if your desk is a mess when he or she empties your trash at night.

The fourth way to change habits is to *remove the cue*. This works well for environment- or tool-based cues. For example, if your phone is set to buzz each time you receive an email, you may get distracted from your classroom visits. Turning off this alert will remove the cue so you have fewer distractions. And if you tend to spend fifteen minutes on email every time you sit down at your desk, simply avoid sitting at your desk whenever it's almost time to get into classrooms.

The fifth way to change habits is to *preempt the cue* with another habit. Some cues may be inevitable, but if you already have another, more powerful sequence in motion, you may be immune to the unhelpful habit loop. For example, if you know staff members will pop by your office with "Got a minute?" queries right before school starts, preventing you from greeting students as they arrive, develop a habit of going outside to greet students a bit earlier. Get ahead of your predictable bad-habit cues, and you can spend more of your day engaged in purposeful activity.

The reason most instructional leaders aren't conducting hundreds of classroom visits per year is that they simply haven't developed the necessary habits. We develop habits gradually, by default, and we come to accept them as normal, inevitable parts of life. As you've seen in this chapter, though, habits have well-defined elements that we can manage and control to achieve more of what we want professionally.

Day 10 Action Challenge: Inventory Your Habits

Identify the key habits that impact your ability to get into classrooms consistently. You may want to consider the following questions for reflection.

▸ What do I most enjoy about visiting classrooms? How can I build these rewards into every visit?

▸ What habits prevent me from getting into classrooms? What triggers these habits?

▸ How can I alter the cues, sequences, or rewards to create more effective replacement habits?

Continue your visits to three classrooms per day, and as you do, look for ways to align your other habits with this key high-performance instructional leadership habit.

.

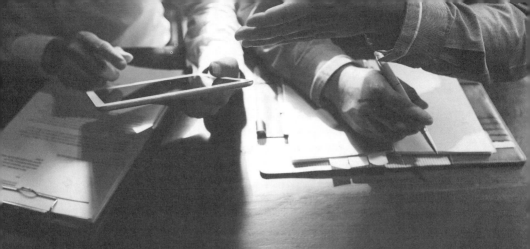

WEEK 3

High-Impact Instructional Conversations

Now that we've explored systems and strategies for making it *possible* to get into classrooms, we'll turn our attention to the next challenge: making it *worthwhile*. If we're honest with ourselves, we don't just avoid classrooms because it's tough to make time; we also avoid visiting classrooms because we haven't found the practice valuable enough to justify the effort involved. In this part, you'll learn how to go beyond the limitations of traditional feedback and have deeper, more impactful conversations rooted in firsthand evidence of classroom practice and linked to your instructional framework.

Going Beyond Data Collection and the Feedback Sandwich

G etting into classrooms on a daily basis is the most transformative habit we can develop because it gives us something most instructional leaders lack: firsthand knowledge about the teaching and learning taking place every day in our schools. When we regularly visit all of our teachers, we get to know them and their students better. We know how they teach, how they run their classrooms, and what they are working on. We know how to support them through our work outside of the classroom, and we know what kinds of professional development they need to continue growing. Just as important, teachers get the benefit of an expert sounding board, another professional who can provide a different perspective and engage in deep conversations about teaching and learning (Danielson, 2015).

Although regular classroom visits do provide rich and valuable information, it's important to define the appropriate audience for that information: teachers and the instructional leaders who work with them directly. Seeing classroom visits primarily as a vehicle for obtaining data to report to third parties—such as district administrators—undermines our overall aims. But if we instead treat ourselves and the teachers we support as the most *direct* beneficiaries of our efforts, and our students as the most *important* beneficiaries, we'll approach our visits differently. Specifically, we'll strive to ensure that we're producing decisional information—actionable insights derived from powerful conversations with teachers—and not just data. But in most schools, data collection is the primary, if not sole, purpose of instructional leaders' classroom visits. In this chapter, we explore how data collection and feedback can undermine professional conversations as well as how feedback can be disconnected from teacher goals.

Learn Why Data Collection Undermines Professional Conversations

Data-driven walkthroughs come from the best of intentions. In a district where principals seldom venture into classrooms, requiring walkthrough data may seem like a reasonable way for a superintendent to bring about change. Getting into classrooms—for any reason at all—is better than staying in the office. And collecting data—whether on student engagement, the teaching strategies that educators use, or any other dimension of teaching and learning—seems like a reasonable way to focus instructional leaders' attention in the classroom and hold them accountable for actually getting into classrooms. If the data can be useful to the district, the thinking goes, even better.

Too often, though, the data go unused, the accountability benefit is minimal, and the very purpose of visiting classrooms is undermined. This is particularly true when data collection focuses on checklists, frequency counts, rating scales, and other quantitative indicators, which provide a very narrow range of information, and capture very little classroom-specific context. This context is essential for having rich, evidence-based conversations about teaching practice, yet it's missing from most data collection instruments.

While it might appear that instructional leaders can collect data while also capturing rich, descriptive evidence—effectively killing two birds with one stone—any effort to collect data has a narrowing effect on the observer's attention. When we know what we're looking for, we tend to focus only on that and miss other important features of a classroom. Our conversations tend to be much richer and more valuable to teachers when we visit with an open mind, rather than a narrow focus on data collection.

For their part, teachers are less interested in data; a 2012 MetLife survey found that fewer than half of high school teachers considered using data to improve instruction to be an important leadership skill (MetLife, 2013). Teachers may even actively resist if instructional leaders do not treat them as the primary beneficiaries of classroom visits. In a major metropolitan district where I've consulted, I learned that administrators visited classrooms on the first day of school with rating forms in hand. Wanting to start the year off right, these well-meaning leaders gave tough but honest ratings to as many teachers as they could visit. Caught off guard and offended by low ratings for rigor and other aspects of practice that may not be the top priority on the first day of school, teachers revolted—and they were right to be angry at this inappropriate use of data. Teachers know that data can be useful, but they're also painfully aware that data can be used against them. Because data collection tends to narrow our focus as observers and because it tends to put teachers in a defensive posture, I recommend that you eliminate data-collection activities from your practice of visiting classrooms.

A Suggestion for Districts Needing Data

If a district truly needs reliable quantitative data, a more cost-effective and valid way to collect them is to train less costly workers—such as graduate students—to design and carry out scientifically valid sampling procedures. School administrators are among a district's most expensive employees—making the data they collect far more expensive—and are also subject to numerous factors that shape how they spend their time. This introduces systematic distortions in sampling; for example, most school leaders spend more time dealing with interruptions in the afternoon, so most of their data collection is likely to occur in the earliest part of the school day.

A carefully designed sampling procedure and trained data collectors can help districts avoid the waste and sampling problems inherent in data collected by administrators. If your district is interested in collecting valid, reliable data on classroom practice, you may want to consider reaching out to local universities, whose graduate students often need real-world opportunities to practice their skills in designing studies and collecting data.

Many districts, of course, use walkthrough data more to hold administrators accountable for visiting classrooms than for any research or improvement purpose. If you want to hold instructional leaders accountable, ask to see their records of classroom visits.

Understand Why the Feedback Sandwich Undermines Professional Conversations

We've all experienced the *feedback sandwich* at some point in our careers. The sequence is probably familiar: a compliment, followed by a suggestion for improvement, and then another compliment. It seems reasonable enough—every lesson has both strengths and weaknesses that the teacher could address, and ensuring that compliments outnumber suggestions is a way to make the experience feel more positive. But as a foundational structure for instructional leadership interactions, the feedback sandwich leaves much to be desired.

First, the feedback sandwich requires the instructional leader to do the bulk of the thinking and deciding. If we want teachers to improve their teaching practice, they must fully engage in this important intellectual work and ultimately make the decisions about how they will change their practice. Conversation is capable of stimulating this level of intellectual engagement (Danielson, 2015). However, the feedback sandwich is not; even if the roles are reversed, asking teachers to reflect on a strength, an area for improvement, and another strength does far less to raise the quality of thinking and decision making than does a rich, evidence-based conversation. Rather than strive to provide compliments and suggestions for improvement, you can stimulate greater growth by engaging teachers in deep conversations about teaching and learning—based on what actually takes place during your visit.

> *Rather than strive to provide compliments and suggestions for improvement, you can stimulate greater growth by engaging teachers in deep conversations about teaching and learning—based on what actually takes place during your visit.*

Second, despite our best efforts as instructional leaders, our compliments and suggestions are seldom useful to the teacher, because they're based on our reactions to a very small portion of a lesson and fail to take into account the teacher's previous decisions and goals. While our evaluation criteria may offer generic descriptions of good teaching that are applicable to all grades and subject areas, there is no perfect lesson, and certainly not one that we can observe in ten or fifteen minutes. We can only judge the quality of a lesson in relation to the teacher's goals for the lesson, and when we visit classrooms, we often don't have enough perspective to make accurate judgments. For example, one issue I encountered frequently as an elementary principal was the varied degree of mastery expected by the end of each mathematics lesson. Our school used a spiral-style mathematics curriculum, in which the teachers introduced concepts gradually over time; as a result, they rarely expected students to master or even achieve fluency with a concept or process in a single lesson. Evaluating the success of such lessons required talking with the teachers about what they had taught previously, what they would teach next, and how well the lesson achieved the teacher's instructional goals for that day.

Finally, the typical feedback approach tends to treat each classroom visit as a self-contained interaction that doesn't leave any loose ends or ambiguity. In reality, our conversations with other professionals are ongoing and aren't always resolved after a few minutes of talking. We may identify issues that require more thinking and discussion or more evidence from future visits. If we resist the impulse to neatly wrap up the work of instructional leadership into a tidy feedback sandwich package, we can avoid giving ill-informed feedback and can better support our teachers in improving their skills over time.

An Unintended Consequence of the Feedback Sandwich

For the small number of teachers who may be facing a negative evaluation at year's end, the practice of giving a written compliment, followed by a suggestion, and then another compliment may provide an unintended consequence: these sandwiches can bolster a teacher's claim that a negative evaluation is unfounded and unfair. If you've packaged all of your written feedback into this format, consider the resulting ratio: two compliments, praising the teacher's strengths, for every suggestion made. If the teacher has implemented your suggestions, yet hasn't improved to a satisfactory level, will your final evaluation withstand scrutiny? Let's say you've visited the teacher's classroom fifteen times, providing a well-crafted feedback sandwich after each visit. If the teacher can provide thirty or more specific compliments you've given, plus fifteen specific suggestions that he or she has implemented, it's likely that your negative evaluation will be overturned—by your supervisor, your human resources department, your school board, or a judge or arbitrator.

CONTINUED ➲

To avoid this situation, avoid the feedback sandwich. Focus your feedback on the evidence itself—what actually happened while you were in the classroom—and if you have concerns, communicate them clearly. Despite its feel-good intentions, the feedback sandwich is an artificial structure that only introduces confusion.

Avoid Feedback Unrelated to Teachers' Goals

Too often, we make suggestions that are irrelevant to teachers because they're unrelated to teachers' goals. Consider the origin of *feedback* as an audio term. Musicians place monitors on the stage so they can hear how they sound through the sound system. This feedback helps them perfect their performance, but it's important to note the source of the sound: the musicians themselves. Feedback is thus an amplified sound signal that returns to its source, not an external critique (Stone & Heen, 2014).

When we give teachers unsolicited suggestions and call them feedback, we're ignoring this basic principle: our feedback must provide teachers with useful information relevant to their goals. Too often, our default approach to providing feedback is to focus on what stands out to us most during our visit, which may or may not be relevant to the teacher's goals. For example, many secondary administrators often focus on student engagement, and while engagement is an important issue, it may not be the right focus for every teacher. Teachers may benefit far more from feedback on other aspects of their practice, which they'll gladly share if asked what they'd like feedback on. This not only leads to more relevant feedback, but also to feedback that teachers are more receptive to.

What teachers want more than feedback is for leaders *to notice them*. They want their instructional leaders to acknowledge their goals, their decisions, and their successes. The 2012 MetLife Survey of the American Teacher (2013) reports that "teachers say that it is most important for a principal to have had experience as a classroom teacher," suggesting that empathy, rather than advice, is what teachers want from their instructional leaders. Noticing what teachers are striving to accomplish is perhaps the most straightforward approach to instructional leadership— all you need to do is enter the classroom with open eyes and an open mind. All too often, though, we enter the classroom with blinders on—blinders created by a narrow focus on data collection or a preoccupation with coming up with a suggestion for improvement. In a successful lesson, it's entirely possible that we won't need to make any suggestions; in fact, our feedback can get in the way of teacher reflection (Danielson, 2015).

Noticing what teachers are striving to accomplish is perhaps the most straightforward approach to instructional leadership— all you need to do is enter the classroom with open eyes and an open mind.

If we want to maximize teacher growth, we must free ourselves from the burden of being the source of that growth, and open our minds to the possibility that our conversations with teachers can be open ended, without tidy conclusions and clear action items. In the best conversations, with the best teachers, we may often find that there's no immediate resolution or action plan for follow-up. This is perfectly normal in conversations—do your conversations with family or friends always end with a suggestion for improvement or a next step? Certainly not—and this lack of closure should be an acceptable outcome in any discussion as complex as those about teaching and learning.

Day 11 Action Challenge: Break the Suggestion Habit

If you are currently collecting data and making suggestions for improvement as part of your practice of visiting classrooms, *stop*—at least temporarily—so you can experience the power of more fully noticing what teachers are striving to accomplish, and so you can engage in more open and authentic conversations. Every time you're tempted to make a suggestion for improvement, think about the teacher as a learner, capable of making self-directed improvement decisions.

You may want to consider the following questions for reflection.

▸ What kinds of information could I share that could lead to greater reflection and change in the teacher's practice, without making a suggestion?

▸ When was the last time I received data that helped me make an improvement decision? What made these data useful?

▸ When was the last time I received feedback that helped me make a change? What characterized this feedback?

12

Facilitating Evidence-Based Conversations

How can we facilitate deep, evidence-based conversations that improve student learning? Conversations with teachers are the best way to help teachers increase the quality of their instructional decisions (Danielson, 2015), and they're also a powerful way to expand your instructional leadership repertoire and skill set. For these conversations to be more than mere philosophizing, though, it's essential that leaders ground them in evidence of what took place in the classroom. In this chapter, we'll explore the key practice of having evidence-based conversations with teachers, so you can ask high-quality, reflective questions that don't put teachers on the defensive. We'll also discuss how to ask genuine questions, ground conversation in evidence, understand the teacher's goals, seek context and withhold judgment, and evaluate practice, not lessons.

Ask Evidence-Based Questions

How can you use what you notice to have rich, meaningful conversations with teachers? The key to higher-quality conversations is to ask better questions about the evidence you've collected. Consider the following sample questions.

- "I noticed that you _____. Could you talk to me about how that fits within this lesson or unit?"
- "Here's what I saw: _____. How does that compare with what you thought was happening at the time?"

‣ "I noticed that _____. How did you feel about how that went?"

‣ "I noticed that students _____. How did that compare with what you had expected to happen when you planned the lesson?"

‣ "I saw that _____. What did you think of that, and what do you plan to do tomorrow?"

‣ "At one point in the lesson, it seemed like _____. What was your take?"

‣ "Tell me about when you _____. What made you choose that response?"

‣ "I noticed that _____. Could you tell me about what led up to that, perhaps in an earlier lesson?"

‣ "I found myself wondering if _____. How does that compare with what you're thinking about?"

‣ "What effect did you think it had when you _____?"

Notice that these questions share several common features. First, they are all genuine questions—you don't know the answers, and you aren't trying to elicit a specific "correct" answer from the teacher. Second, they're all grounded in specific events that transpired during the visit—even though you may not yet have enough context to fully understand what you saw. Third, these questions position the teacher's goals for the lesson—cross-referencing the evidence to the instructional framework—as the main criterion for success. Fourth, they assume that you aren't yet ready to offer a critique of what you observed—at least, not until the teacher has filled in essential context about what happened before the lesson, the purpose of the lesson, and what will happen next. Finally, these questions frame the visit as the focus for discussion, but not as a discrete performance that you can evaluate or score as a measure of the teacher's overall performance. We'll explore each of these concepts in the remainder of this chapter.

Ask Genuine Questions

If we want to have real, professional dialogue with teachers, it's essential for our questions to be real questions about which we're genuinely curious, not didactic or leading questions that imply a single correct answer.

While questioning may hold some appeal as a way of helping teachers arrive at specific conclusions on their own, it's likely that they will interpret such questions as condescending and a waste of time. Teachers prefer that instructional leaders simply say what they intend to say directly, rather than beat around the bush or drop hints. For example, if you believe that the teacher should have used a particular instructional strategy, a series of leading questions is unlikely to help the teacher arrive at the desired conclusion without some degree of frustration. Instead, it might be more helpful to note the strategies the teacher did use, and then ask about the rationale behind each strategy. If you want to make a suggestion, make it directly, but often you'll find that your suggestions become unnecessary once the teacher has had a chance to discuss the lesson with you.

If we want to have real, professional dialogue with teachers, it's essential for our questions to be real questions about which we're genuinely curious, not didactic or leading questions that imply a single correct answer.

Genuine questions are the foundation of professional conversation because they require the instructional leader to listen and to withhold judgment while learning about the teacher's goals for the lesson and the context surrounding the observed portion of the lesson. It may be impossible to hide the assumptions behind a question—for example, if you think a particular aspect of the lesson was unsuccessful, that's likely to be apparent to the teacher—but genuine questions allow you to remain open to the possibility that your assumptions are incorrect.

To ensure that you're asking genuine questions, first ask yourself, "Do I think I already know the answer to this question?" If so, don't ask it— instead, ask a more open-ended question that raises the subject without leading the teacher to a specific answer. Or, if you do want to raise a specific issue, simply state your thoughts directly, rather than trying to word them as a question.

Ground Conversation in Specific Evidence

Visiting classrooms—even briefly—can lead to impactful conversations between teachers and instructional leaders because it provides firsthand evidence about the teacher's practice. Rather than discuss teaching in the abstract, we can share our observations of the specific learning activities that took place during the visit, and present them to the teacher for discussion.

It's important to understand that teachers start out at a disadvantage in evidence-based conversations because they don't have the luxury of stopping to observe and take notes while they're busy teaching. As an outside observer, you're uniquely able to gather evidence of what takes place during a lesson, so it's essential that you pay close attention to what you see and hear, and then share what you notice with the teacher, providing evidence, in as descriptive a format as possible. This evidence serves as the basis for substantive conversations about teaching and learning. What you notice and share with the teacher should be as low-inference and literal an account of what transpired during your visit as possible. The goal is not to make suggestions for improvement, but to provide a shared foundation for discussion.

Although you won't take written notes in your first two rounds of classroom visits, after a very brief visit, you can verbally recount what you saw, especially if you have a chance to talk right away. By your third cycle, you'll be ready to have more substantive conversations, and you'll have built enough rapport with staff to avoid causing consternation when you show up and start taking notes. When you begin taking written notes in your third cycle of visits, share them with the teacher immediately, and refer to them as you talk. When observing teachers who may be especially anxious about your presence in the classroom, you may want to promise in advance to share your notes to reduce potential fears about what you may be writing.

Many instructional leaders have been trained to take low-inference notes that describe what's taking place in the classroom as literally as possible—for example, noting what the teacher says and does, what the students say and do, how much time elapses, and so forth. If these notes are in a personal shorthand or another hard-to-decipher format, it will help to write out more comprehensible narrative descriptions of what took place, or to simply recap verbally what the instructional leader observed, without judgment.

An Advantage of Providing Low-Inference Notes Rather Than Suggestions

The advantage of providing low-inference notes, instead of written suggestions, is that it's fast and there's no potential for misunderstanding. If you write down what you see and hear during your visit, there's no additional work to do after you leave the classroom, so you can get on with your day, and circle back to talk with the teacher when your schedules align. In the meantime, the teacher will receive a copy of your notes, and won't worry that you've drawn the wrong conclusions.

If you are accustomed to handwriting your notes, consider using an electronic device to increase the speed and accuracy of your documentation, while also making it easier to share your notes with teachers. Rapid typing may make teachers nervous, so be sure to explain what you're doing, and share your notes with the teacher immediately to avoid keeping him or her in the dark about what you noticed.

When you share your notes and have evidence-based conversations with teachers, you're making it extremely clear what you saw during each classroom visit. Your written records may become very important as a source of evidence at the end of the year, when you prepare formal evaluations. However, you'll want to avoid referring to your notes as "evidence" in your conversations with teachers, because the word *evidence* has a negative and overtly evaluative connotation. To keep the conversation focused on learning, simply call your notes *notes* or perhaps a *narrative* or *running record* of what you saw during your visit.

Another option, which you should only consider if teachers are open to the idea, is to record video during the visit, and to use this video as a source of evidence for the follow-up discussion. While there's no substitute for face-to-face conversation, many administrators find it helpful to have teachers review and annotate their videos before they meet, so face-to-face time can focus on discussion rather than on reviewing evidence. Visit www.instructionalleadershipchallenge.com/video for current recommendations on video tools that support high-performance instructional leadership.

Understand the Teacher's Goals

Our conversations with teachers should focus on genuine, evidence-based questions rather than feedback because it's only against the teacher's goals for the lesson that we can truly evaluate its success or failure. If we seek first to understand what teachers are striving to accomplish when we visit classrooms, our conversations will be far more productive and professionally rewarding than if we drop by only for the purpose of delivering a feedback sandwich.

As an instructional leader, you may prize the role you play in upholding high standards for teachers, and you may find it impossible to avoid passing judgment the moment you walk into a classroom. These judgments are not necessarily wrong, and you should not disregard them. However, they are premature, and they should not serve as the basis for your conversation with the teacher except in the most extreme situations, such as a class that is out of control due to poor classroom management.

Why are our snap judgments necessarily premature? In short, because teachers bear professional responsibility for determining how they'll use class time to help students learn. Instructional leaders who believe it is their job to dictate how every moment of the day is spent will soon find themselves exhausted by the need to micromanage and supervise teachers at all times. If we accept that teachers are responsible for making decisions about how to spend class time, it's essential that we take their goals into consideration when drawing conclusions from a brief observation.

For example, an instructional leader who is new to the practice of visiting classrooms daily may be surprised that many students fail to fully grasp a new concept that the teacher has introduced in a mathematics lesson. However, in many mathematics programs, teachers introduce concepts gradually over a series of lessons, and do not expect students to attain mastery within a single class period.

In other situations, the events of the week may influence how a class spends a particular brief period of the day; for example, returning student work may not be the most interesting class activity for an instructional leader to observe, but it's still necessary. Ultimately, it's the teacher's goals for the lesson that determine whether it was successful or not. Trying to discuss a lesson without clarity about the teacher's goals will lead only to frustration.

Seek Context and Withhold Judgment

Because most classroom visits are so brief, it's essential to withhold judgment about what we see until we have more context; a learning activity only makes sense in relation to what happened before and what will happen after it. As you discuss your observations with teachers, be sure to use the questions earlier in this chapter (page 105) to establish the context of what you observed. Too often, instructional leaders jump straight to their suggestions for improvement and don't give teachers a chance to explain what they've already done and what they plan to do next. This leads to wasted effort and reduced trust. When instructional leaders make suggestions without seeking context, they imply that teachers need to be told what to do and simply comply, rather than think for themselves; this failure to view teaching as professional work is sure to insult experienced teachers. In addition, it's likely that the teacher has already done more thinking than the instructional leader about the lesson, and it's likely that he or she has already considered the suggestion—and potentially rejected it for perfectly valid reasons.

Trying to discuss a lesson without clarity about the teacher's goals will lead only to frustration.

We have the greatest impact on teachers' thinking when we withhold judgment and refrain from making suggestions until after we've fully explored the meaning of the lesson in its larger context.

Evaluate Practice, Not Lessons

Finally, it's essential to understand that when we evaluate teachers, we're evaluating their overall practice, not specific lessons—much less small portions of lessons. In our zeal to promote high standards of professional practice, we have too often turned the briefest of classroom visits into opportunities for evaluation. This is both unfair and unwise.

In the grand scheme of things, it does not particularly matter how teachers use any given five- or ten-minute period of class time; what ultimately matters is the long-term impact teachers and their instruction have on students and their learning. I've often heard classroom visits described as a *snapshot* or *dipstick* that indicates what takes place the rest of the time, when the observer isn't in the room. This can be useful in identifying troubling patterns quickly, but it's important not to extrapolate from single incidents. For example, I once visited a high school classroom with the school's assistant principal, and we saw that students were watching a cartoon. We asked a few students what they were watching and why, and it was clear that the teacher had decided to have a free period for students, and the cartoon was playing merely to keep students entertained and quiet. The assistant principal set up a meeting with the teacher for later in the day to discuss expectations for how to use class time and to ensure that showing cartoons did not become a regular occurrence.

In the grand scheme of things, it does not particularly matter how teachers use any given five- or ten-minute period of class time; what ultimately matters is the long-term impact teachers and their instruction have on students and their learning.

While the assistant principal was right to question the teacher's decision to show a cartoon in lieu of purposeful learning activities, she was also right to meet with the teacher to discuss the situation, rather than simply issue a reprimand. It would not be fair to suggest that this teacher always showed cartoons or never used class time effectively. Had students worked hard for weeks to earn this free period? How much class time had students spent watching cartoons? How purposeful was this teacher's decision to show a cartoon on that particular day? Our brief visit didn't provide enough information. While the visit and follow-up conversation resulted in important corrective feedback for the teacher, it would not be accurate to view our visit as a dipstick indicative of daily practice, and it would not be fair or accurate to write the teacher's overall evaluation based on this single visit.

Most instructional leaders simply are not in classrooms enough to discern consistent patterns about teacher practice. As you implement the high-performance instructional leadership model, you'll gather much more evidence over the course of the year, and you'll start to develop a better sense of what constitutes typical practice for each teacher. However, the fact remains that the purpose of teacher evaluation is to evaluate teachers' *overall* practice, not the success of a single lesson or part of a lesson. Teaching is complex work that doesn't take place in smooth, equal increments each day; observing for ten minutes doesn't tell us how effective a fifty-minute lesson is overall, and observing a whole lesson doesn't tell us how much students will learn over the course of the year. It's only through talking with teachers repeatedly, inquiring about their instructional choices, and gathering evidence over time that we can make valid, defensible judgments about teacher performance. We can later use the evidence to support an argument in an evaluation—but we often don't know what our argument will be until we see a pattern. We can avoid sending the wrong message early on by focusing on conversation, not evaluation, after each classroom visit.

Day 12 Action Challenge: Refer to Evidence

As you talk with teachers today, refer more specifically to what you saw and heard (but don't call it *evidence*). Send the message that you're paying attention not to judge or evaluate, but to understand and learn. Use the questions in this chapter to have more evidence-based conversations. Though you won't take written notes and share them with teachers until your third cycle, you'll want teachers to understand that you're paying attention, not just making an appearance.

You may want to consider the following questions for reflection.

- What did I notice in a classroom today that I immediately judged in my mind? Did I keep this concern to myself, or did I bring it up with the teacher?

- What would need to change in the teacher's thinking or practice to address that concern?

- What implications does this concern have for our school, and for the action I need to take as a leader?

13

Bringing a Shared Instructional Framework Into the Conversation

When we're talking with teachers about their teaching, how can we ensure that the conversation is constructive? As instructional leaders who take our commitment to improving student learning seriously, it's our responsibility to ensure that teachers are challenging themselves, not just explaining themselves and expecting to continue with the status quo. Like many principals, I've had conversations with teachers who seemed more interested in defending their current practices than in finding ways to grow. Even with the most growth-minded teachers, it can be awkward to keep the focus on improvement without becoming overly critical—and the better the teacher, the more hypercritical it can feel to find areas for growth. I've tried countless approaches to helping teachers honestly reflect on their practice and identify ways they can improve, including approaches that worked, and others that completely backfired. My most important discovery has been the power of bringing a third party—a shared instructional framework—into the conversation. In this chapter, we'll explore the limitations of opinion-based conversations, and you'll learn how to use your instructional framework as an arbiter to avoid conflict, as well as strategies for handling disagreements about performance. This in-depth discussion of your instructional framework will help make conversations with teachers more rigorous and more constructive, with less conflict.

Understand Problems With Opinion-Based Conversations

In the typical one-on-one conversation after a classroom observation or brief visit, the teacher and instructional leader have differing incentives—even if both care a great deal about improvement. It's in the teacher's best interests to demonstrate competence and end the conversation as quickly as possible. From the teacher's perspective, the instructional leader does not know as much as the teacher about what the teacher needs to do next in order to grow (Danielson, 2015). The instructional leader also wants to demonstrate competence, and thus usually makes suggestions for improvement based on what he or she felt the teacher could have done better. This requires a vision for what good practice looks like and how well the observed practice—the evidence from the visit—aligns with that vision. When teacher and instructional leader don't have a clear, shared understanding of what good practice looks like, even the most evidence-based conversation hinges on little more than personal opinion.

Overreliance on personal opinion and personal judgment sets the teacher and instructional leader at odds because the teacher's tendency is to strive to demonstrate competence, while the instructional leader's mandate is to identify gaps in the teacher's competence—areas in which the teacher falls short. The more the teacher becomes defensive and resistant to change, the more the instructional leader goes on the offensive and becomes less willing to listen and learn from the teacher's experience. This dynamic undermines the improvement potential of the conversation—but you can avoid it if a shared instructional framework plays the role of arbiter.

Use the Instructional Framework as an Arbiter

When teachers and instructional leaders share a common framework defining good teaching practice, conversations can focus on aligning documented evidence with the criteria that the framework lays out. Instead of a tug-of-war over whether the teacher's practice is good enough, the conversation becomes a process of triangulation. Because the instructional leader no longer plays the role of judge, the conversation can become collaborative and nonconfrontational.

Of course, instructional leaders who happen to be evaluators are, ultimately, charged with judging teacher practice. These judgments, backed by the evidence instructional leaders have gathered over time and aligned with the instructional framework, are an important means to hold teachers accountable for their performance and ensure that all students have access to high-quality learning experiences. Within a single conversation, though, emphasizing the instructional leader's role as an evaluator triggers teacher defensiveness and inhibits the kinds of professionally rewarding conversations that are possible with the high-performance instructional leadership model.

With a shared instructional framework in place, a conversation about classroom evidence is essentially a three-way discussion—with the framework serving as the third "person" in the conversation. The teacher and instructional leader can review the evidence and ask, "How does this align with our framework's definition of good teaching?" The specific answers the framework provides are a key resource for improvement. We turn now to describing the nature and scope of instructional frameworks.

> *With a shared instructional framework in place, a conversation about classroom evidence is essentially a three-way discussion—with the framework serving as the third "person" in the conversation.*

Understand the Components of Your Instructional Framework

Your overall instructional framework involves several nested sets of expectations and descriptions of good teaching practice. It's based on sources including—but not limited to—your teacher evaluation system, professional development, and adopted curricula, which work together to provide teachers and instructional leaders with a set of common expectations for ideal teaching practice. While your instructional framework is a collection of documents and resources rather than a single document, it's essential that its major components are available to teachers in writing. You should have gathered these documents together during the Day 2 Action Challenge (page 22), and you may want to refer to them as you read the remainder of this chapter.

Teacher Evaluation Criteria

At the most basic level, the first source of your instructional framework is your *teacher evaluation criteria*, which may be written into state law or your teacher employment contract. These criteria often include areas such as classroom management, planning and preparation, professional responsibility, and skill in conveying information clearly and accurately to students. Historically, the sources of these criteria have defined them very loosely, within relatively broad categories, leaving administrators substantial discretion in how to interpret and apply them. For example, Washington state law requires principals to evaluate teachers in eight areas, including "interest in teaching pupils," without specifying what constitutes interest in teaching pupils, how leaders might judge it, or how they might discern varying degrees of interest in teaching pupils (Washington State Legislature, n.d.).

Beginning in 2009, many states overhauled their teacher evaluation criteria in response to the U.S. Department of Education's Race to the Top grant program, which—in addition to many other changes—resulted in more specific, leveled indicators for teacher performance (National Center for Education Evaluation and Regional Assistance, 2014). Many states and localities chose to use Danielson's (2007) *Enhancing Professional Practice: A Framework for Teaching* as the basis for their new evaluation criteria. These clear, descriptive criteria provide teachers and instructional leaders a common language with which to discuss evidence of classroom practice, and because they include explicit, leveled performance descriptors, they can serve as arbiter in discussions about professional skill. The same is true for other modern frameworks that go beyond the *satisfactory* or *unsatisfactory* paradigm by providing four-tiered performance indicators. Thanks to these new tools, our conversations with teachers can focus on the evidence and on facilitating teachers' reflection on practice with regard to the criteria. But formal evaluation criteria aren't the only aspect of your instructional framework.

Professional Development Strategies

A second source of common expectations is your school or district's history of *professional development*, which may include specific instructional strategies that staff have been trained to use. For example, when I was a new teacher, my district ran a multiyear professional development initiative across all subject areas and grade levels to train teachers in using specific literacy strategies. When professional development strategies become districtwide expectations, they can serve as excellent reference points in instructional conversations. In order to serve as part of your instructional framework, though, instructional strategies need to meet several criteria.

When professional development strategies become districtwide expectations, they can serve as excellent reference points in instructional conversations.

First, all staff must receive thorough training in a clear set of common strategies. Second, the district must clarify and communicate expectations for using the strategies. Third, and most crucially, the district must develop leveled performance indicators; otherwise, instructional leaders and teachers will focus on quantity rather than quality. The more administrators require the use of specific strategies without attention to quality, the more teachers will be incentivized to engage in gamesmanship to show observers what they want to see, without making good use of the strategies the rest of the time.

Quality indicators can be as simple as teacher-developed rubrics for each strategy; unlike overall evaluation criteria, leveled performance indicators for instructional strategies can be extremely specific and lend themselves to the evaluation of individual lessons or segments of lessons.

Adopted Curricula

A third source of common expectations, which may not apply uniformly to all staff, is *adopted curricula*. Many literacy and mathematics programs, for example, require specific approaches to instruction that differ in important ways from typical approaches. While these expectations will be relevant only to teachers in certain grades and subjects, they are among the richest available reference points for instructional conversations because they're so specific to what educators are teaching—and how they're teaching it—on a day-to-day basis. Particularly when teachers are learning new approaches, it's invaluable to discuss their practice with instructional leaders and triangulate classroom evidence with the leveled performance descriptors in their curriculum guides.

Regardless of the origin of a shared expectation in your instructional framework, it's inadequate to focus on *whether* you've observed specific behaviors. Instead, your focus should be on the *quality* or level of performance you observe, and that's why it's so important for an instructional framework to distinguish between varying degrees of proficiency and quality. If your current expectations for teaching practice don't include leveled performance descriptors, start working with teachers at the team or staff level to develop rubrics for practice. You may find it easier to establish rubrics during professional development so teachers can distinguish between poor, mediocre, acceptable, and exemplary practice as they learn about a new strategy, rather than after they've been implementing it—perhaps poorly—for some time.

Finally, it's essential to clarify the circumstances under which teachers should use a given strategy. While we often pay attention to whether teachers are using preferred strategies, and we sometimes consider the skill with which they use them, we too seldom consider when they're appropriate and when they're not. When I was a new teacher, I would learn new strategies in weekend professional development sessions, and then use them in class the following week, for no reason other than that I thought I was supposed to apply what I was learning. A clear vision for instructional practice should provide teachers with clarity about their options for meeting students' needs, not a laundry list of strategies to implement.

Make Sense of the Instructional Framework and Grain Size

A robust instructional framework doesn't always lend itself to use in brief classroom visits, because many of the nuances that allow us to distinguish between varying levels of performance aren't directly observable; we can only explore them through evidence-based conversations. While it's common for districts to require administrators and other instructional leaders to conduct classroom walkthroughs with observation checklists or other instruments, this approach differs in critical ways from the high-performance instructional leadership model. When we observe teachers, a checklist of the behaviors and strategies they exhibited is among the least useful types of feedback we can provide. Instead, use your instructional framework to discuss *quality*—the teacher's level of performance—based on specific evidence, and with attention to grain size.

Grain size refers to the appropriate unit of analysis for a given element of an instructional framework. For example, some overall evaluation criteria cover the teacher's practice over the course of the entire year, such as professional behavior and communication with parents. The rubrics (such as Danielson, 2007) that address such aspects of practice are not intended to produce judgments based on a single incident or even a small number of incidents; they're designed to evaluate the overall pattern of the teacher's practice. It's a mistake, therefore, to use year-long evaluation rubrics to judge the quality of individual lessons.

For curriculum-specific instructional strategies, the grain size may be much smaller, and it may be entirely appropriate to evaluate the quality of, say, a mini-lesson in a literacy class, based on an ultra-specific rubric in the curriculum guide. For individual instructional strategies, the grain size may be even smaller; for example, a leader can assess the practice of using proximity and eye contact to deal with student misbehavior, rather than resorting to verbal reprimands, in the few seconds that it takes the teacher to notice misbehavior, make eye contact with the student, and move closer to the student while continuing the lesson.

Grain size matters because it's critical that we evaluate the various elements of practice when we have an appropriate amount of information—not prematurely, as we're often tempted to do when we face the considerable time pressures common to our work. The concept of grain size also helps us recognize the vast amount that we don't know about the teachers we work with. A teacher who fails to clarify the purpose of a lesson on one observed occasion is not necessarily a teacher who *always* makes the same mistake; the teacher is the best judge of his or her typical practice.

If teachers are to be the primary evaluators of their own practice in our instructional conversations, what role do we play as instructional leaders? Our role becomes one of facilitating the conversation to keep it on track, to keep it close to the evidence, and to keep it honest with regard to the levels of performance we're seeing.

In your third cycle of visits and beyond, a conversation might go like this: after visiting a classroom, you share your written (ideally, typewritten) notes with the teacher, so you both have full access to the evidence about what took place in the classroom. You then ask genuine questions about the evidence (see the sample questions in chapter 12, page 105), and engage the teacher in conversation about how the lesson went relative to the teacher's own expectations. When appropriate, you link specific evidence from your notes to the criteria in the instructional framework—while keeping the issue of grain size in mind. The teacher may identify aspects of the lesson that he or she could have approached differently and may identify action steps to take before the next visit. Or, you might make suggestions to guide the teacher's reflections or provide ideas for next steps. If the teacher cites evidence for a certain performance indicator, you should ensure that the evidence fits the level of performance that the teacher has identified, and guide the teacher to an honest and accurate assessment of his or her practice.

Will this result in clear follow-up steps and a satisfying sense of closure? Not always. The nature of professional conversation is that it's ongoing— just as you may have ongoing conversations with family members that don't reach a resolution or result in action-oriented decisions each time you discuss them. Respecting the professional nature of teaching as a process of exercising professional judgment requires that we allow for the possibility that some issues will remain unresolved. These open topics can lead to even richer subsequent conversations, resulting in decisions that are ultimately more accurate and more effective in improving performance.

Learn Strategies for Handling Disagreements About Performance

What if a teacher reviews the evidence you provide, reviews the relevant aspects of the instructional framework, and arrives at an inflated view of his or her own practice? This is a very common and rational response; after all, evaluations can have a real impact on teachers' employment status. A few basic strategies can keep conversations on track, even when the teacher is exaggerating his or her level of performance relative to the instructional framework.

As a starting point, we must recognize that teaching is a complex, long-term endeavor, and not something that only occurs in a single class period while an observer is in the room. While the evidence we gather during our visits to classrooms is a critical foundation for our conversations, it doesn't tell the complete story, so we must approach our instructional conversations with a degree of humility and openness. To put it more bluntly, we should always be open to the possibility that our harsher judgment is wrong and the teacher's rosier self-assessment is right. We must also help teachers recognize that they don't have total knowledge of how their lesson went and what each student experienced; we may have noticed weaknesses in the lesson that the teacher was unable to see in the moment.

Closing the gap between teacher self-assessments and our judgments is a matter of sharing information and perspectives through conversation and written evidence. That's why it's so critical to take detailed notes and to share them with the teacher to establish a common understanding of the basic facts. Then, when you start to discuss the evidence, you can make purposeful use of specific terminology from your instructional framework to guide the teacher toward your perspective. For example, if you're discussing higher-order questioning strategies with a teacher who believes she possesses exceptional skill in this area, you can use terminology from your framework's descriptions of *satisfactory* and *distinguished* practice in the area of questioning, and it will become clear, in the course of your conversation, which descriptors best fit the evidence. Even so, how can we determine whose judgment we can trust in any given situation? We should recognize that we don't always have enough information to address a certain criterion; we may wish we had perfect information on our entire framework, but often, we'll have just a fraction of the information we'd like.

If we do have enough information to draw conclusions about the teacher's level of performance with regard to specific criteria, it works best to identify the level of performance and then pull specific instances from your written documentation to serve as evidence. This may require several attempts, and in the course of your conversation, you may realize that the teacher was right, or the teacher may realize that you were right. Either way, it helps to use the specific, leveled language of your framework as much as possible, because this will aid in triangulation. For example, if you're triangulating your conclusion that a teacher is *distinguished* in Danielson's (2007) domain 2, component D, *Managing Student Behavior*, you may want to use terms such as *proactive* and *subtle* throughout your discussion, as these terms appear in the *distinguished* column of the rubric.

If you can't come to agreement on a final rating, that's fine; keep in mind the grain size issues discussed previously. You don't need to evaluate teachers on their final evaluation criteria after every visit; that will take multiple observations and conversations over the course of the year. If you remain in disagreement, let the teacher know where you stand, communicate that you understand that the teacher's perspective differs, and don't try to force a resolution.

Day 13 Action Challenge: Use Instructional Framework Language

Return to the various evaluation documents, professional development programs, curricular resources, and other sources that will contribute to the shared instructional framework that you gathered on day 2. You'll want to bring these documents with you as you converse with teachers during your third round of visits.

In the meantime, as you make your first two rounds of visits, talk with teachers about what you've observed in their classrooms, start to use the language of your framework to describe what you see, and help teachers use this same language in their reflections.

You may want to consider the following questions for reflection.

- ‣ What staff professional development has provided us with the most expectations and language in recent months?
- ‣ What specific curricula am I most familiar with and least familiar with? What professional vocabulary drawn from these curricula am I already using?
- ‣ What instructional activities are hardest for me to describe in precise framework language?

14

Developing Skills for High-Impact Conversations

The more we engage in open-ended, evidence-based, framework-linked conversations with teachers, the better we'll get at facilitating these conversations and ensuring that they're productive. This requires considerable skill in asking authentic questions, active listening and paraphrasing, probing for deeper reflection, and following up to support teachers as they take action. The best way to develop these skills, though, is simply to get started.

Many instructional leaders hesitate to start because they haven't experienced the rewards of visiting classrooms and talking with teachers—even if they've gone through the motions. If we're going to make a sustained habit of visiting classrooms and having professional conversations, we must structure the process to ensure that it's professionally rewarding; otherwise, we'll find reasons not to stick with it. In this chapter, we'll discuss how to have professionally rewarding conversations, how to provide feedback in response to teacher requests, how to respond when teachers become defensive, how to have impactful conversations, and how to accept nonclosure.

Have Professionally Rewarding Conversations

Conversations are professionally rewarding when they both *provide information we need* and *lead to better decisions*. This is equally true for

Conversations are professionally rewarding when they both provide information we need and lead to better decisions.

instructional leaders and teachers. If we examine the conversations that we *don't* find professionally rewarding, it's easy to see that they are often missing one of these factors for one or both parties.

Consider a conversation in which it's your goal to make a suggestion for improvement. Does this provide the teacher with information? Yes, if it's linked to evidence from the classroom. But does it lead to better teaching decisions? Often, no—the suggestion serves more as a critique of the teacher's past decisions than a means of improving the teacher's ability to independently make better decisions on related matters in the future. If that's the case, the teacher doesn't stand to benefit from the suggestion, and the conversation will feel like a distraction at best, and an intrusion, or even a mild form of harassment at worst—far from the professionally rewarding ideal that we may envision (Danielson, 2015). A professionally rewarding conversation must lead to better decisions, and it must provide decisional information to the teacher or the instructional leader—ideally both.

The best information comes from conversations in which the teacher does the majority of the talking. If we want our conversations with teachers to result in improvement, we must allow teachers to remain in the driver's seat; they should evaluate their lessons' success against their own goals, referencing your shared instructional framework. We learn about how teachers think from listening, and teachers grow more when they're the ones doing the majority of the thinking and talking (Danielson, 2015). As a leader, you'll make better decisions for your school—both operational and improvement decisions—when you know, in depth, how each teacher thinks and makes instructional decisions.

Listen When Teachers Ask for Feedback

Some of the best instructional leadership interactions take place when teachers ask for feedback on specific aspects of their teaching. A first-grade teacher once invited me to observe while she was trying a new vocabulary strategy, and it was one of the most professionally rewarding conversations I've ever had. As a result of the invitation, observation, and ensuing conversation, I was able to make a better decision about additional professional development for the teacher, for which she was requesting funding.

When teachers ask for feedback, it's important for instructional leaders to understand that they aren't simply inviting open-ended criticism; they're asking for information on specific aspects of their practice that they are trying to improve. Providing feedback upon request is a responsibility we must take seriously and handle carefully. The feedback we provide must be based on the teacher's goals, and must take into consideration the context surrounding what we see. We must accept that these goals may not relate directly to school-level improvement goals.

If a teacher has invited you to provide feedback on a specific aspect of his or her practice, should you limit your feedback to that topic? Unless you identify a serious problem, yes. Avoid the tendency to insert your own priorities or raise every issue that comes to mind, and limit your feedback to the topic the teacher has identified. If you have serious enough concerns that you'd issue a directive—in other words, if your goal is not to help the teacher engage in reflective practice, but instead to compel an immediate change in behavior—then provide clear direction, and save the requested feedback for another visit. Teachers cannot receive both directives and reflective feedback at the same time, because directives trigger defensiveness.

Understand How to Handle Teachers Who Become Defensive

Defensiveness is a sign that we've triggered teachers' natural instincts for self-preservation. Being observed by another adult—especially one who influences the teacher's final evaluation—is a potentially threatening process, and this should not surprise or frustrate us. I sometimes hear instructional leaders complain that their teachers are being defensive or don't want feedback, but they're placing the blame on the wrong party.

It's not the teacher's job to avoid being defensive; it's the instructional leader's job to create a climate safe for reflective practice. Traditional feedback does the opposite, and that's why we must avoid it whenever possible.

It's the instructional leader's job to create a climate safe for reflective practice.

We have a choice: we can either keep teachers focused on reflection and growth in our conversations, or we can become directive and focus on changing behavior rather than thinking. We can obtain compliance, or we can raise the level of teachers' thinking, but we can't do both. If we don't like the response we're getting, it's our responsibility as instructional leaders to change what the teacher is experiencing from us.

Have Impactful Conversations

An impactful conversation about teaching and learning doesn't have to be complicated; in fact, good conversations are often simpler than feedback sandwich conversations because they're more natural. Here is a set of suggested steps for impactful, authentic conversations rooted in evidence of classroom practice and linked to a shared instructional framework.

First, ask for permission. "Do you have a minute to talk, or would later be a better time?" This is a classic approach telephone salespeople use because if the person doesn't actively give his or her consent to talking, he or she may not be fully tuned into the conversation, and it won't have the intended impact. If it's not a good time, set up a time to talk later—perhaps during the teacher's preparation time or the following day.

Second, allow the teacher to choose a focus. An open-ended question like, "So, how did you think it went?" may not be specific enough, and it may prove difficult to wrest the conversation back to a productive topic. However, it can be very helpful to ask a specific question to discern the teacher's goals for the lesson and whether they were achieved. You might ask, "How did what students were able to get done compare with what you had in mind?" Or, you might ask, "What outcome did you have in mind for that part of the lesson?"

After you've established the teacher's purpose, you'll have a clearer sense of where you should refer to specific evidence from your observations.

At this point you can say something like, "So you wanted to make sure students understood how to solve the problems on last night's homework. I saw that you went around checking students' papers—what did you see as you checked their homework?"

You can then continue the discussion using the sample questions for better feedback from chapter 12 (page 105). In your third cycle of visits, as you refer to specific events that you have documented in your notes, make reference to your instructional framework so the teacher can evaluate his or her own practice against the criteria in the framework.

Don't panic if the teacher seems to have an inflated view of his or her own practice. The focus should remain on evidence; as you gather more evidence and engage in more conversation using the language of your framework, disagreements tend to disappear. If the teacher presses his or her case for a high self-rating that you remain skeptical of, you can indicate that you didn't see everything you'd need to in order to fully agree, but that you'll be back in a few days and can look for further evidence.

This conversational flow may not work well if you have serious concerns. If you plan to provide directive feedback, see chapter 15 (page 131) for guidance on handling tougher conversations.

Accept a Lack of Closure

After talking with the teacher for a few moments, you may find that an interruption forces the conversation to end without a clear conclusion. Or, you may find that there's not a clear takeaway; if the teacher is able to respond to your questions, and you don't have any suggestions, it may feel anticlimactic to end with a simple, "Well, it's been great to stop by. See you later!"

But if our conversations are to be authentic, we must allow them to end in just such an unceremonious fashion. Normal conversations don't always end with clear action items; they may, but they don't have to. When you visit your doctor for a checkup, the main takeaway is often to come back in six months for a follow-up appointment. When you visit a teacher and there isn't an obvious next step, it's fine to depart with a simple statement like, "Thanks for taking the time to talk with me. See you again in a few days!"

You should always strive for clarity; don't leave the teacher guessing what you are thinking. But you may find that your conversations continue over email, after staff meetings, or in the copy room. This is the way human conversations naturally evolve, and we should accept this lack of closure in our professional conversations with teachers.

Day 14 Action Challenge: Engage Without Defensiveness

As you continue your daily visits to classrooms today, inquire more deeply into teachers' goals and thoughts on their lessons. As you encounter teachers who are typically defensive about their practice and resistant to suggestions for improvement, use the process I have described in this chapter to engage them in deep conversation about their practice without triggering their usual reactions. Write down the questions you find to be most effective for these teachers, and make a note of which conversations seem to have the greatest impact. Remember not to start taking written notes until your third cycle of visits, after you've had a chance to build rapport with each teacher and clarify your intentions to the whole staff.

You may want to consider the following questions for reflection.

‣ When have I experienced a lack of closure in conversations with teachers so far?

‣ What questions or phrases have worked well for presenting evidence to teachers without making them defensive?

‣ What do I hope teachers find most rewarding about our conversations?

15

Handling the
Toughest Conversations

Most teachers thrive under the high-performance instructional leadership model because it allows them to have rich, professionally rewarding conversations with instructional leaders, and the greater frequency of classroom visits provides a much more accurate representation of their practice than the formal observation process. However, there will always be a small percentage of teachers who resist any administrative presence in their classrooms, or who have inflated views of their abilities. How can we maximize the impact of our classroom visits, even in the most challenging circumstances? To answer that question, we'll look at what to do when you're not welcome, how to discourage the impromptu performances, how to keep conversations on track, and how to maintain rigor and accuracy when discussing practice.

React Thoughtfully When You're Not Welcome

When you start to visit classrooms on a more regular basis, it's important to follow the process I outlined in chapter 4 (page 35) to set expectations, establish trust, and avoid triggering the predictable fears that teachers naturally tend to have. Even so, some teachers will resist any type of instructional leadership visit to their classroom. This resistance may take several forms, each of which we'll consider in turn.

First, if a teacher tells you he or she doesn't want you to visit at all or insists that you notify him or her in advance when you plan to visit, it's necessary and appropriate to use your positional power to justify your presence—but you should do so thoughtfully. If you simply insist that you have the right to visit classrooms at any time, you'll likely encounter further resistance such as a refusal to talk, increased involvement from union representation, or complaints of harassment. These forms of resistance are no small matter, but they're easier to prevent than respond to.

Instead of emphasizing your *right* to be in any classroom at any time, focus on your *responsibilities* as an instructional leader. The primary benefit of visiting classrooms on a regular basis is the decisional information you obtain from seeing teachers at work and talking with them about their practice. If a teacher objects to your unannounced visits, calmly explain your need for firsthand information about students and their learning and about teachers and their teaching. Emphasize that it's your job to be in classrooms and that you can't fulfill your responsibilities effectively without being in classrooms.

If a teacher objects to your unannounced visits, calmly explain your need for firsthand information about students and their learning and about teachers and their teaching.

Second, teachers may resist talking with you during or after your visits. In many cases, this resistance comes from the grueling schedule most teachers face; they may simply not have time to talk with you and accomplish everything else they'd planned for the day. We want to have impactful conversations with teachers, but we don't want to prevent them from using the restroom, being ready for their next class, or keeping an appointment they've made with someone else. When you approach a teacher to talk about your visit, start by asking if he or she has a moment to talk. If not, ask when a better time would be, and follow up then. This small courtesy can go a long way.

If it becomes apparent that the teacher's preferred time to talk is *never*, explain that you want to make sure you understand the context of what you saw—for example, what happened before and after you visited. Most teachers are eager to explain themselves and ensure that others see their practice in the best possible light, so this will resolve the majority of issues.

For the small number of remaining teachers who continue to resist your visits or follow-up conversations, it may be necessary to clarify your expectations for all staff and how they align with your commitment to visit all classrooms regularly and talk individually with each teacher about what you see. Teachers need to know you're not singling them out, and when they see that you're visiting their peers as well, they'll tend to avoid singling themselves out by resisting.

Ultimately, you may need to state in unambiguous terms that your visits are a condition of the teacher's employment; if he or she would prefer not to be observed or talk about his or her practice, he or she will need to find another place to work. However, if you encounter this level of resistance from more than two or three people, it's more effective to address it as a trust issue, rather than rely on positional power. Trust is essential for achieving the benefits of the high-performance instructional leadership model, so it's best to avoid pulling rank with all but your most resistant teachers.

Discourage the Impromptu Dog-and-Pony Show

A more common challenge to productive classroom visits is that teachers may change their behavior—or even the activities that students engage in—the moment you walk into the room. One of the primary benefits of unannounced classroom visits is that they allow you to see what's taking place under more typical circumstances than a preplanned, formal observation (Marshall, 2013). Even so, if teachers think they know what you want to see, they may strive to put on a miniature dog-and-pony show whenever you arrive.

One teacher I worked with didn't complain when I started to visit her classroom regularly, but she undermined my purpose for visiting (perhaps unintentionally) by stopping the class, announcing my presence, and asking the class to greet me in unison: "Good morning, Mr. Baeder!" She then described what students were working on, explained its purpose, and asked specific students to share their work with me. This prevented me from understanding what had been taking place prior to my arrival, so I explained my purposes for visiting and asked that the class continue with their work whenever I visited. My visits became much more productive, and our conversations improved markedly.

Most teachers won't stop their lessons when you visit if you've set expectations carefully. Instead, you may find that they're putting on a show to ensure that you see what they believe you're hoping to see. This, too, is a matter of setting expectations; if you see teachers scrambling to use a certain strategy the moment you walk into the room, it's likely because you (or someone else in your school or district) set the expectation that teachers use that strategy on a regular basis. It's entirely rational, then, for them to put on a show for you; teachers know you only observe them for a tiny fraction of their total instructional time, and they know they won't get credit for using the strategy unless you see it during your brief visits.

To discourage this behavior, avoid telling teachers that you're looking for a specific strategy or practice when you visit. It may be tempting to try to collect data on the use of specific practices when you visit classrooms, but in most cases, this simply does not work; you stand a small chance of seeing any particular strategy in brief visits, and if teachers know what to expect, they'll strive to ensure that you see it. Note that this is a different matter from having an instructional focus, such as rigor, on which you center your conversations with teachers; since rigor is a characteristic of instruction rather than a specific behavior, such a focus is less likely to distort what you see when you visit.

Keep Conversations on Track

Some teachers may welcome your visits and the opportunity to talk with you, yet still divert the conversation into noninstructional matters. This may be a defensive mechanism—to avoid talking about areas where they may need to make improvements—or it may simply be a chance for the teacher to vent or get your help with a problem. For your post-visit conversations with teachers to be productive, it's essential that they remain rooted in the evidence of what actually took place in the classroom.

For teachers who tend to push the conversation in noninstructional directions, it may be helpful to start by sharing what you noticed and treating those observations as the starting point for the conversation. You may want to avoid opening with a general comment like, "How's it going?" because the teacher may see it as an invitation to introduce any topic he or she has in mind.

Once you're talking about the evidence itself, you may encounter a second type of diversion: excessive focus on what students should be doing differently, rather than the teacher's instructional decisions. The more you attempt to judge the success of the lesson, the more teachers will feel pressure to defend themselves by shifting responsibility to students. While it's certainly true that learning requires effort from both the teacher and the students, we want these conversations to improve teachers' ability to make high-quality instructional decisions, not to assign blame for any shortcomings in the lesson.

To avoid student-blaming diversions, use the precise, leveled language of your instructional framework to describe specific incidents that arose in the lesson. While it's not our goal to rate the lesson, it's important that we obtain our descriptive language from a shared instructional framework so we can establish clarity about the story the evidence is telling. For example, if you notice that transitions are taking too long during one of your class visits, you might glance at Danielson's (2007) domain 2, component C, *managing classroom procedures*, and notice that the phrase "Much instructional time is lost due to inefficient classroom routines and procedures" appears in the *unsatisfactory* column. While you should avoid giving a rating of the lesson, you can guide your conversation with the teacher in the right direction by using the framework's leveled language. You might first say, "Looking at my notes, I'm noticing that it took seven minutes for students to put away their materials and return to their seats. Let's look at our framework and see what it says about classroom routines and procedures. What do you think might make transitions more efficient?" Then, give the teacher time to review the framework and identify the relevant portions of the rubric. This will keep responsibility where it belongs—with the teacher.

To avoid student-blaming diversions, use the precise, leveled language of your instructional framework to describe specific incidents that arose in the lesson.

Maintain Rigor and Accuracy in Discussing Levels of Practice

When you use specific, leveled descriptors from your instructional framework to discuss the evidence from a visit with the teacher, the teacher's incentive is to cast his or her own practice in the best possible light; after all, there's no reason the teacher should help you obtain evidence of poor or mediocre performance. Does this mean that every conversation needs to become a back-and-forth argument about the quality of the lesson?

Since these arguments focus on rating what the teacher has already done rather than informing future decisions, they're counterproductive given the purposes we've established. To avoid this tug-of-war, we can emphasize clear descriptions of the evidence, using the leveled language, without actually rating the lesson. If you and the teacher can't agree on what language from your framework is most appropriate, you can agree that more evidence would be helpful, and you can plan to discuss the same topic after your next visit.

Day 15 Action Challenge: Prepare for Challenging Conversations

Identify the teachers who are engaging in the most challenging behaviors during your visits and conversations. What types of resistance are you seeing—opposition to your presence? Reluctance to talk? Defensiveness? Inflated self-perceptions? In your next conversation with a challenging teacher, keep the focus on the evidence from your visit, and start to make clearer, more explicit references to your instructional framework.

You may be tempted to visit these teachers less often in order to avoid these challenging conversations. To resist this tendency, continue your visits to class-rooms according to the rotation you've been following, and don't allow yourself to skip anyone. Remember not to begin taking written notes until your third cycle of visits; in the meantime, simply pay attention during your visits, and be prepared to share what you noticed in the follow-up conversation.

You may want to consider the following questions for reflection.

- What will most likely be my next challenging conversation? Who will it be with, and what will we need to talk about?

- What are the most common emotions I have when observing in the classroom of a teacher with challenging behaviors?

- How can I best be genuinely helpful to this teacher the next time we talk?

WEEK 4

High-Performance Instructional Leadership Enhancement

If daily classroom visits and substantive, evidence-rich conversations with teachers are to become a sustained part of your instructional leadership practice, you'll need to develop a long-term plan for helping your practice evolve so you can avoid fatigue, develop solid habits, and sustain the benefits of this work. In this part, I discuss how you can make your conversations with teachers more substantive, actionable, and useful as you make decisions about individual teachers and how to lead your school.

16

Building Your
Feedback Repertoire

To get started with the high-performance instructional leadership model, you won't initially need to record or provide written feedback; just get into classrooms, pay attention, and talk with teachers. However, when you finish your second cycle of visits, you'll be ready to begin capturing accurate documentation so you can have richer, more evidence-based conversations with each teacher. In this chapter, we explore how to expand and capitalize on the rich, nuanced vocabulary you use to talk about practice with teachers.

Over time, you will want to increase your ability to artfully carry on these conversations face to face, and even supplement them with email when appropriate given the topic and your relationship with the teacher. Written discussion gives both you and the teacher more time and space to delve into deeper issues—which may not happen in a quick chat between classes. Written feedback will also become much more important as you begin to prepare formal documents such as observation reports and final evaluations. Thus, here we take a deeper look at writing high-quality feedback, learning the vocabulary of your curriculum, keeping your feedback repertoire accessible, structuring your thinking with templates, building trust, noticing and documenting what matters most, and using your feedback repertoire in conversation.

Write High-Quality Feedback

If you find it challenging and time consuming to write high-quality feedback, you're not alone. Writing high-quality feedback is cognitively demanding because it requires that you both pay attention to the most salient issues from the classroom, and that you find precisely the right words to help advance teachers' thinking and practice—without doing all the thinking for them. There are no shortcuts to doing this intellectual work, but the strategies that follow will allow you to get far more mileage out of the writing you produce.

The key is to build a repertoire of carefully crafted language that you can use over and over again whenever it's appropriate. Some instructional leaders feel an obligation to write all of their feedback from scratch, but you shouldn't feel bad if you use the same words and phrases over and over again. In fact, you should embrace reuse—squeeze every drop of utility from every phrase you craft. When you're talking about something specific that you see over and over again, it's natural that you'll return to certain language that you've used in the past. Any time you've already crafted just the right phrases for a particular situation—especially those that link especially well to your instructional framework—reuse them with pride. For example, if you often notice teachers skillfully redirecting students who are off-task, you might look at Danielson's (2007) framework and notice under domain 2, component D, *managing student behavior*, the phrase "Teacher monitoring of student behavior is subtle and preventive" (in the *distinguished* column). If you draw on this language in a written formal observation summary, you might craft a sentence such as "Mr. Smith skillfully redirects students who are off-task using subtle strategies that do not disrupt the rest of the class, and he relies on preventive strategies such as eye contact and proximity to help easily distracted students stay focused. For example . . ." Crafting such a sentence can be difficult and time consuming, but since the evidence that follows will link this statement to Mr. Smith's specific actions, this sentence can be reused with other teachers. Simply include relevant, specific evidence, and you can honor each teacher's practice without having to write everything from scratch.

Learn the Vocabulary of Your Curriculum

When you provide written feedback, strive to use the precise language of your curriculum and other aspects of your instructional framework. Remember, your framework is more than just your evaluation document, which may be too broad to address the finer points of each specific subject area. Look to other shared sources of professional language, including your curriculum, shared instructional practices, and other professional literature for words and phrases to use in your feedback.

This vocabulary can become quite extensive; the more you participate with teachers in their subject-area professional development, the more you'll be able to speak the precise language of their discipline. When I was a new principal, I had no experience as an elementary literacy teacher; my background was in secondary science, so the teaching of reading and writing was far outside my areas of expertise. Knowing that I'd need to understand literacy instruction in order to lead my school effectively, I participated alongside teachers in all of the training in our new reading and writing curriculum. Because our school spanned six grade levels, I wasn't able to sit in on every session or master every nuance of each grade's curriculum, but I was able to pick up on most of the professional vocabulary and core structures of this curriculum.

I also obtained a copy of the teacher's guide for each grade level, so I'd have a reference on hand if I wanted to understand more about the design of a particular unit. As I visited classrooms, I would sometimes review the teacher's guide to understand the context of the lesson within a larger unit, and on many occasions, this knowledge stopped me from giving unhelpful feedback, such as suggesting changes that wouldn't make sense within the scope and sequence of the curriculum. Too often, when we give low-quality feedback, it's because we don't know enough about the curriculum teachers are using. To overcome this problem, attend as much content-area professional development as you can, review the teacher's guides, and delve into the standards with teachers.

Too often, when we give low-quality feedback, it's because we don't know enough about the curriculum teachers are using.

Keep Your Feedback Repertoire Accessible With a Phrase Database

When studying a new language—say, to prepare for an international trip—it's essential to learn how to actually put sentences together, and not just memorize individual words. We must know the grammar and syntax of any language we hope to use effectively. But recalling both the words and the most common constructions can present a significant challenge. Native speakers of a language develop a vocabulary in the tens of thousands of words, and while we may not face quite so great a challenge in mastering the language we use to talk about instruction, it's still tough.

But you don't have to rely on your memory alone to master the language of instructional leadership; you can rely on reference documents and technology, especially for written feedback. And the more you do, the more you'll have the right words at your disposal when you're having face-to-face conversations with teachers.

Teacher observation apps, such as Repertoire (www.principalcenter .com/repertoire) and TeachBoost (www.teachboost.com) can help you develop and manage your professional vocabulary. These web-based apps allow you to import or build databases of criteria and phrases or snippets that you can reference while writing. If you're writing an observation report for a teacher who, like Mr. Smith in the example earlier in this chapter, skillfully and subtly redirects students who are off-task, you can search the app for the phrase "off-task," and anything you've written previously using that phrase will appear in the search results. You can then insert this phrase into the current observation report with a single click. You can also save language from your instructional framework in this database; for example, if you've imported the text of Danielson's (2007) framework, a search for the phrase "classroom management" would return several results from domain 2, *classroom management*, component C, *managing classroom procedures*. Then, if you need to craft a new statement to fit the situation, you can refer to these criteria as you write, and you can save the new phrase for future reuse.

Over time, using a phrase database helps you in two ways. First, it greatly speeds up the writing process by allowing you to quickly reuse phrases and sentences from your ever-growing language bank. Second, the ability to find and refer to both instructional framework language and your previous writing helps you write with greater precision in each new situation. For example, if you're writing about a teacher's use of subtle redirection with an off-task student, referring to your phrase database may lead you to realize that the teacher is also using preventive strategies, which you may not have noticed in the moment. Developing a sharper eye will help you have more substantive and impactful conversations with teachers.

Structure Your Thinking With Templates

Even with a vast repertoire of phrases at your fingertips, you may find that *structure* is the most challenging aspect of writing high-quality feedback; if so, you may find it helpful to create a few templates to prestructure your thinking for various situations. Templates differ from checklists or forms in that they're a tool for planning your writing, not a way to replace or minimize it. When you're finished filling out a form, it still looks like a form, but when you've successfully used a well-designed template, it looks like any other piece of writing—as if you've written it from scratch.

A template can give an overall structure to your comments; for example, if you have a standard salutation, a few sentence starters (such as, "I noticed . . .," "Students were . . .," "You were . . .," and "I'm wondering . . .") and a standard closing, you'll have a flexible, solid structure you can use to recap any lesson—simply fill in specific evidence and questions. For example, you might follow this structure to quickly write an email as follows.

> Dear Mr. Smith,
>
> It was great to see your students at work today during fourth period earth science [*salutation*]. I noticed that students were working diligently on their lab reports, and you were circulating to keep everyone on track [*I noticed, students were, you were*]. When Dylan put

his pencil down and seemed to be daydreaming, you didn't call attention to him, but subtly moved closer and made eye contact to remind him to get back on task [*evidence*]. I'm wondering what other strategies you're finding to be effective in helping him stay on task [*question*]—could we catch up during your sixth period prep or after school?

—Justin [*closing*]

As you can see in this example, this template could easily be reused for another teacher or another visit to the same teacher, with different evidence and questions filling in the blanks. To the teacher, it reads like a normally composed email, but it's much faster to write because of the predetermined format.

Another example of a flexible, powerful template is Jon Saphier's *claim, evidence, interpretation, and judgment* (CEIJ) format (Saphier, 1993), which is useful for writing final evaluations (see chapter 17, page 158). The ten questions for evidence-based feedback in chapter 12 (page 105) can also serve as templates for written feedback. While templates contain general-purpose structures rather than specific language, they can also be saved in your phrase database to speed up your writing.

Build Trust With Consistency, Not Canned Feedback

You may be worried that using templates and having a go-to repertoire of words and phrases will result in multiple teachers getting feedback containing the same language. That's not a bad thing; if the situations you're describing are similar, your comments should be similar. Consistency will build trust when teachers compare notes—as long as your comments don't appear canned. Your writing won't appear canned if it addresses the teacher and the situation specifically. Strive to match your comments to the precise situation, and continually broaden your repertoire so you can be as specific as possible.

The best way to avoid a canned feeling in your writing is to phrase your feedback in second person, so you're addressing the teacher directly rather than talking about the teacher as if to a third party. This will help you avoid the stilted tone of your evaluation framework and help your writing come across more conversationally. For example, "The teacher selected a clear objective for the lesson" sounds more canned than, "You selected a clear objective for the lesson." Final evaluations may require you to write in third-person language, but since your feedback is directed toward the teacher, you should write it in second person, to the teacher.

Another way instructional leaders fall into the trap of canned feedback is to use a phrase that isn't quite right for the situation. It's fully appropriate to reuse your writing when it fits well, but if it's not quite right, customize it. Don't describe two lessons that aren't the same as if they are. For example, if another teacher, Mr. Jones, redirects an off-task student, but does so in a humorous rather than a "subtle and preventive" way, don't try to reuse what you wrote for Mr. Smith; craft a new statement, or modify an existing statement until it fits the evidence.

Notice and Document What Matters Most

When you're taking verbatim, transcript-style notes during a classroom observation—formal or informal—they should include only factual descriptions of what you observed, not your own interpretations or judgments. You'll share these notes with the teacher and have a conversation about what you noticed, so there's no need to include questions, suggestions, or ratings in the notes. Your goal while observing in the classroom is to document, not to evaluate. But that doesn't mean your instructional framework plays no role while you're in the classroom.

When you're observing a lesson, your instructional framework plays a critical role in helping you notice what matters most. A classroom full of students is an enormously complex environment, one that even a dozen video cameras couldn't fully capture. Your ability to *notice* is your most essential skill as an observer, and this ability derives mainly from your knowledge of your instructional framework. Without a deep knowledge of your instructional framework, you'll tend to

Your ability to notice is your most essential skill as an observer, and this ability derives mainly from your knowledge of your instructional framework.

focus on what the teacher is doing and what the teacher wants you to focus on—or perhaps what the worst-behaving students are doing—and you'll miss the nuances of the classroom that can serve as the best grist for discussion and growth.

For example, if your instructional framework specifies that the best classroom discussions involve students asking questions and responding to one another's comments—not just answering the teacher's questions—you'll know to focus on the teacher's facilitation strategies, not just the quality of the teacher's questions.

As you capture what's taking place in the classroom, allow your instructional framework to guide you to document the most salient events and comments. You can't document everything—even during whole-group instruction—so focus your notes on what you plan to discuss with the teacher so you have ample evidence.

Use Your Feedback Repertoire in Conversation

As you develop a larger and larger repertoire of feedback words and phrases, you'll find it easier and less awkward to use the specific terminology of your instructional framework in conversation with teachers. However, you may find that you hardly ever use an entire criterion as written; for example, "The teacher uses a variety of engagement strategies to involve all students in class discussions" is too awkward to use conversationally, so you might say, "Let's talk about the engagement strategies you used to get students involved in the discussion about the causes of the Revolutionary War." The goal is not to parrot your evaluation criteria verbatim in your conversations with teachers, but to develop a rich, nuanced professional vocabulary that allows you to describe classroom evidence with great specificity.

Day 16 Action Challenge: Find Reusable Language

Think about your last few conversations with teachers, and start to identify language you may want to use again. You won't want to start taking notes until your third cycle of visits, but think through your most recent conversations, and if you sent follow-up emails or left other written comments, review them now.

You may want to consider the following questions for reflection.

‣ What phrases did I use that I notice myself using over and over?

‣ What salutations do I tend to use in email or other written correspondence? Are there any circumstances in which I would use a different salutation?

‣ What existing documents (for example, last year's evaluations) might contain language that I could save and reuse?

17

Balancing Your Formal Evaluation Responsibilities

As you develop the habit of visiting classrooms daily, you'll realize that you're collecting far more information about teacher practice than most principals have at their disposal. Because you're in classrooms so frequently, you'll be able to write much better final evaluations based on far more evidence. Though our focus in the high-performance instructional leadership model is not primarily on evaluation, the evidence you collect and discuss with teachers is immensely useful when writing formal evaluations. In this chapter, we'll explore the delicate relationship between your informal classroom visits and your evaluative responsibilities as a school administrator. We'll discuss how every aspect of your teachers' teaching should be considered fair game, recall contractual restrictions on informal observations, differentiate between high-stakes and low-stakes evaluations, and learn to allocate formal evaluation time with the 80:20 rule. We'll also delve into how to close the gap between high-stakes and low-stakes teachers, and learn the *claim, evidence, interpretation*, and *judgment* (CEIJ) method for writing rock-solid evaluations. If you're not formally in an evaluative role, this chapter will help you distinguish your visits from evaluative visits and protect the purpose of your work with teachers.

Consider Everything Fair Game

As teachers, we learn to loathe hearing the question, "Will this be on the test?" from our students. We want students to internalize the idea that everything is fair game when it comes to their learning. Similarly, we want our teachers to be "on" all the time, not just putting on a good show for their formal observations (Marshall, 2013). Our students need teachers to be operating at 100 percent every day, not just once or twice a year.

You may prefer to mentally draw a distinction between instructional leadership activities that support growth, such as informal visits and conversations, and those that are part of the official evaluation process, such as prearranged formal observations. Certainly, if you're an instructional coach, or in another role which does not involve evaluating teachers, it's essential to create a clear boundary around your coaching work so teachers know you will not report on their challenges and weaknesses to their evaluator; this is a basic requirement of coaching that you should respect as the foundation of your professional relationship.

But if you're a teacher's evaluator, the separation between support and evaluation exists only in your mind; legally and ethically, you cannot draw a strict distinction between information you'll use for supporting teachers' growth and information you'll use for conducting their formal evaluations. As I've emphasized throughout this book, the chief benefit of visiting classrooms daily is acquiring decisional information. It's inevitable that you will use some of this information, directly or indirectly, to make evaluation decisions.

For this reason, it's essential to avoid the claim—at any point in the process—that your visits to classrooms are nonevaluative. As an evaluator, every interaction you have with teachers informs your appraisal of their practice and, ultimately, your official evaluation of their performance.

We now explore how to handle evaluation evidence for underperforming teachers. If we proceed with due caution in these situations, we'll be more than prepared for the rest of our evaluations.

Remember Contractual Restrictions on Informal Observations

Depending on your teacher contract, it may or may not be officially permissible to use informal observations in official teacher evaluations. For example, collective bargaining agreements may stipulate that only *formal* classroom observations can be used as evidence in a formal evaluation. If you're in a similar situation, don't despair. If we understand why these restrictions are often in place, we can find appropriate ways to work within them.

The main purpose of distinguishing between formal and informal observations is to prevent "gotcha" observations in which supervisors lack the appropriate context to understand what they're seeing. You'll recall from chapter 13 (page 120) that individual lessons aren't the appropriate *grain size* or unit of analysis for teacher evaluations, yet traditionally evaluators only observe most teachers once or twice a year. Without a chance to brief the observer on the context and purpose of the lesson, teachers may understandably fear that evaluators will misjudge their efforts.

If you aren't able to use evidence from informal visits to classrooms, check your teacher contract and district policies carefully; it may be that you can conduct *unannounced* formal observations, which probably are not too dissimilar from the visits you're already making. You may have to stay a certain minimum amount of time, or provide a written report, or have an official post-observation conference with the teacher within forty-eight hours, for example. If a small adjustment to your process for visiting classrooms can enable these visits to count in the final evaluation, it may be more than worth the extra effort. For an ambitious model that replaces all formal observations with unscheduled mini-observations, see Kim Marshall's (2013) excellent book *Rethinking Teacher Supervision and Evaluation* (see also Mini-Observations, page 26).

Another approach that may work—again, depending on the specifics of your teacher contract—is to document your visits not through formal observation reports but through letters of concern or reprimand when you encounter misconduct issues. There should be some provision for this in your school's policies; for example, if you saw a teacher behaving inappropriately toward a student in a hallway, the policy would not prevent you from addressing this situation as a supervisor simply because it wasn't part of a scheduled, formal observation. If the policy specifically prohibits using evidence from your unscheduled classroom visits, addressing *misconduct* may be an effective approach with extremely low-performing teachers. Our focus in this book is on teacher *practice* rather than misconduct, but when their practice is extremely poor, teachers are much more likely to resort to approaches that fall within the scope of misconduct—such as yelling at students while struggling with classroom management.

If you have any concerns about teacher underperformance, don't delay in speaking with your supervisor, human resources representative, or legal counsel.

If you have any concerns about teacher underperformance, don't delay in speaking with your supervisor, human resources representative, or legal counsel. It's essential to begin with a clear understanding of the contractual or legal restrictions on using evidence from your informal visits in formal evaluations.

Even under the strictest limitations, informal visits to classrooms can help you make informed decisions about where to spend more of your time during the formal observation process. If you can't use any evidence from informal visits in formal evaluations, simply schedule additional formal observations whenever you discover that you need more evidence about a particular teacher's practice.

Differentiate High Stakes and Low Stakes

As you gather more and more information from your informal visits—whether you can use this information in official evaluations or not—you'll gain clarity on which teachers are doing well and which are doing poorly. This information can help you classify each teacher evaluation as either *low stakes* or *high stakes*. You'll likely have many low-stakes teachers who will not be at any risk of a negative evaluation due to a strong track record of consistent performance. You'll have a smaller number of teachers who are marginal, and a few who are missing the mark by a large margin. These struggling teachers, as well as new teachers whom you do not yet know very well, will be in the high-stakes category.

It might seem that the fairest approach would be to defer all judgment until the end of the year, so you'll have an equal amount of evidence for each teacher, and so you can judge each teacher impartially according to this evidence. In reality, though, you'll have a strong sense of how each teacher is doing long before the end of the year, and even if you can defer formally rating your teachers, it's impossible—and unwise—to defer all judgment. Putting off judgments about teacher performance until the end of the year is intellectually dishonest, wasteful, and ineffective. It also results in a great deal of unnecessary documentation for high-performing teachers and results in an inadequate amount of evidence for low-performing teachers.

Instead, I recommend a more focused approach. As a result of your frequent classroom visits, you'll have a strong intuitive sense about each teacher's level of performance, as well as a great deal of written documentation. It's unlikely that you'll miss warning signs about the teachers you deem low stakes, because you'll continue to visit their classrooms regularly and engage them in ongoing conversations about practice. The more you know about teachers' thinking and decision making, and the more frequently you've seen their teaching, the clearer a sense you'll have of their true level of performance. And because you're evaluating teachers' overall practice rather than individual lessons, it will only strengthen your relationships with and impact on lower-performing teachers to have them on your high-stakes list.

> *The more you know about teachers' thinking and decision making, and the more frequently you've seen their teaching, the clearer a sense you'll have of their true level of performance.*

What does it mean for an evaluation to be *high stakes*? It means you must adequately prepare for the possibility that the teacher may not meet expectations and may thus need to receive an unsatisfactory evaluation. This demands a more intense level of evidence collection and effort, and requires that you take all feasible steps to address any poor teaching you've seen. Too often, evaluators vastly underestimate the amount of work it takes to respond to ineffective teaching, and—since there's a high degree of uncertainty involved—we often devote this effort to the *wrong* teachers.

To err on the side of safety, mentally categorize roughly 20 percent of teachers—marginal performers as well as new teachers who haven't yet established themselves—as having high-stakes evaluations. This categorization exists in your mind only; you shouldn't communicate it to the teacher in any way. After all, it's only a preparatory step, so you can focus your evaluation efforts where they're likely to have the most impact. In most cases, you'll see enough improvement or evidence of satisfactory practice that you won't actually pursue dismissal for these teachers. The remaining 80 percent of your teachers can be safely deemed low stakes. This 80:20 ratio seems to be the sweet spot, balancing effort and uncertainty. If you were to treat only 5 percent of your evaluations as high stakes, you might fail to identify several struggling teachers, and fail to collect adequate evidence about their practice. On the other hand, a 50:50 ratio would lead to an untenable amount of wasted effort; low-stakes evaluations should and must consume less of your time and effort. If you categorize 80 percent of your evaluations as low stakes and 20 percent as high stakes—and if you visit classrooms daily, as I advocate throughout this book—you'll stand a very high chance of gathering all of the evidence you need without too much wasted effort.

In contrast to this approach, most evaluators focus on only the teachers they consider the absolute worst—typically one or two per year. This often leads to shock and frustration when other teachers—who may have been promising new hires, or may have flown beneath the radar for years—emerge late in the school year as the biggest concerns. Again, teachers shouldn't experience any negative consequences from your closer scrutiny, because it's merely a categorization in your mind. There's no harm in being prepared.

Allocate Formal Evaluation Time With the 80:20 Rule

Once you've categorized your teachers as high or low stakes, how should you allocate your instructional leadership time and effort? In implementing the high-performance instructional leadership model we've discussed in this book, you'll want to spend roughly equal time on *informal* visits with each staff member—both to ensure that you gain a good balance of information and to maintain the perception of fairness. When you start visiting classrooms more frequently, some teachers may feel that you're targeting them, so it's essential to demonstrate that you're spending roughly equal time in each classroom.

You should more purposefully target your *formal* evaluation efforts, though, to ensure that the process achieves results that justify the effort, and this means investing dramatically more time and effort in writing your high-stakes evaluations. Compared to informal classroom visits, formal evaluation activities should only take up a small proportion of your overall instructional leadership time, and it's essential to allocate this time, overwhelmingly, to the teachers who are most at risk of receiving a negative evaluation.

Plan to spend 80 percent of your formal evaluation time on high-stakes evaluations, and the remaining 20 percent on the low-stakes evaluations. You'll likely observe each teacher for the same, required amount of time (for example, thirty or sixty minutes, depending on norms and policies in your district), so the difference is mostly in your behind-the-scenes effort. This may seem extreme—if you have twenty teachers and plan to spend one hundred hours per year evaluating them, following the 80:20 rule means spending eighty hours on your four high-stakes evaluations (twenty hours per teacher), and only twenty hours on your sixteen low-stakes evaluations (an hour and fifteen minutes per teacher). Consider the alternative, though: when we fail to effectively evaluate our lowest-performing teachers, we have to repeat the process the following year, and in the meantime, students suffer. Twenty hours is a reasonable estimate of how much time it takes to conduct a high-quality, high-stakes evaluation—though it may require more time to carry out additional steps such as probation and dismissal. And ideally, those twenty hours result in dramatic improvements that forever change the teacher's career, so you're not wasting this time even if the final evaluation is positive.

How can you use this differentiated allocation of time effectively? Throughout most of the year, there will be little difference in how you approach high-stakes and low-stakes teachers' evaluations. If you normally observe for an hour when completing formal observations, observe both your high- and low-stakes teachers for an hour; teachers should not notice a difference. But you'll want to invest dramatically more time and effort in assembling and writing about your evidence. Take extra care to avoid making statements that aren't supported by your evidence—especially encouraging remarks, such as "Keep up the good work," that may be interpreted later as indicating a lack of performance problems.

As you obtain more information, you can differentiate your approach further. If a new teacher you've placed in the high-stakes group turns out to be outstanding, you can mentally recategorize her as your confidence grows, and spend less time on documentation and writing. On the other hand, if your concerns about struggling teachers grow as you spend more time in classrooms, you can increase the time and effort you put into documentation and initiate other support and evaluation activities, such as plans of improvement, as needed. Be sure to consult with your supervisor, human resources contact, or legal counsel for any teachers you believe may need to be placed in a path toward dismissal.

Most of the extra effort you invest in high-stakes teacher evaluations will come at the end of the year, unless your concerns are serious enough to justify earlier action.

Close the High-Stakes Evidence Gap

As you approach the end of the year, it's essential to review your evidence for each high-stakes evaluation and ensure that you have enough evidence to make a strong case.

As you approach the end of the year, it's essential to review your evidence for each high-stakes evaluation and ensure that you have enough evidence to make a strong case about each teacher's performance. By the end of the year, many teachers you initially categorized as high stakes will have demonstrated their abilities to your satisfaction, so can recategorize them as low stakes. For more marginal teachers, it may be unclear exactly how you should rate the teacher in your final evaluation, so it will take extra time, effort, and diligence to assemble your evidence and make your decisions. Long before any formal evaluation documents are due, start marking a copy of your school's formal evaluation tool with the evidence you have, so you can determine what evidence you lack. You may want to print a copy of your evaluation rubric for each teacher and write dates on each section to indicate when you've collected evidence relevant to that criterion.

Then, as you conduct your remaining formal observations, you can ensure that you collect enough evidence and schedule additional observations as needed. You may find that your standard schedule of observations is adequate and that you can best devote your additional effort to mining these observations more deeply for evidence in multiple areas. If you've taken detailed, low-inference notes and develop a high degree of skill in linking them to your instructional framework, you'll have plenty to work with. It's fortunate that this extra investment of time and effort can take place entirely in writing, without causing the teacher any undue alarm. Remember, you're only categorizing evaluations as high stakes in your own mind, so if the evidence reveals that a teacher is actually performing at a satisfactory level, you can avoid the stress and conflict inherent in pursuing a negative year-end evaluation.

However, for the teachers who do seem to be marching quickly toward a negative evaluation, it's often wise to conduct several additional observations. By this stage, it will become obvious that the teacher is receiving more scrutiny, so it's appropriate to inform the teacher of your concerns and start outlining clear expectations for improvement in specific areas. Because you've limited the time you're spending on the other 80 percent of your evaluations, you'll have more time and mental energy for these challenging evaluations. While a full exploration of how to deal with challenging evaluations is beyond the scope of this book, the approach outlined should give you the two things you need most: time and evidence. Because you're spending so much time in classrooms on an informal basis, you can approach your low-stakes evaluations with a great deal of confidence, allowing you to complete the formal evaluation process very quickly. Because you'll start collecting written evidence during your third round of classroom visits, you'll have a sizeable body of documentation about each teacher's practice, even if you don't conduct any additional formal observations. This approach allows you to allocate additional time to high-stakes evaluations as needed, and to further modify your approach as you learn more about each teacher's performance. An alternate means of differentiation is to use the CEIJ format with your high-stakes evaluations.

Learn the Claim, Evidence, Interpretation, and Judgment Format for Writing Rock-Solid Evaluations

When preparing a high-stakes negative evaluation, the *claim, evidence, interpretation,* and *judgment* format (Saphier, 1993) is invaluable. This time-tested approach was passed on to me when I was an administrator in Seattle Public Schools, and I've developed the following descriptions to help you craft clear, well-supported arguments about teachers' performance. You can use CEIJ to write extraordinarily strong positive evaluations—for example, in recommendation letters—but for our purposes in this chapter, we'll focus on negative evaluations, because low-stakes evaluations generally don't justify the time required to write a thorough CEIJ-format evaluation.

When preparing a high-stakes negative evaluation, the claim, evidence, interpretation, *and* judgment *format is invaluable.*

The foundation of the CEIJ format is clarity—it requires that you eliminate all ambiguity from your writing. Rather than require readers to draw their own conclusions from the evidence you present, the CEIJ format walks the reader step by step through a straightforward and logical argument.

The *claim* is an unambiguous statement about the teacher's overall practice in reference to a specific evaluation criterion. For example, a *claim* might be, "Mrs. Smith does not deal effectively with student misconduct and has failed to establish a classroom climate conducive to learning. As a result, students spend significant time off task and engaged in conflict."

You must back this claim, of course, with solid *evidence,* such as, "For example, on 1/31, I observed a brief exchange in which two students exchanged verbal insults, followed by a fifteen-minute attempt on Mrs. Smith's part to get the students to ignore each other. During this time, instruction completely stopped, and the conflict was not resolved. In another incident that I observed, on 2/17, three of the five groups spent their group work time arguing over who would do the work and completed less than half of the assignment in the designated time."

The verbatim evidence—notes from the observation—should already be in the teacher's possession, so there's no room to dispute the facts. However, you may want to withhold an overall interpretation of this evidence from individual conversations throughout the year and only articulate it in the final evaluation, since you're evaluating the teacher's overall practice. For example, the *interpretation* might read, "Because Mrs. Smith does not deal with student misbehavior in a timely and authoritative fashion, the classroom environment makes it difficult for students to learn—even for students who are attempting to ignore distractions."

While it may be premature to make such generalizations after a single observation, by the end of the year, the pattern should be clear enough to summarize in this way, and then pass *judgment* on: "Therefore, in Professional Practice Standard 4, Classroom Management, Mrs. Smith's practice is best characterized as Level 1, Unsatisfactory."

While the CEIJ format includes a degree of redundancy, a few clarifications are in order. First, the *claim* is a statement about the teacher's characteristic practice, whereas the *interpretation* describes the impact of this practice on student learning or other relevant outcomes. Second, while the *claim* makes a summary statement about the teacher's practice, it's more descriptive in nature than the *judgment*, which is simply a rating based on the evaluation criteria. By separately articulating each of these aspects of the argument using the CEIJ format, you can craft a compelling argument that is virtually impossible to dispute, assuming you have the necessary evidence.

If you find it difficult to start with a clear claim, it may help to go through several drafts, starting with your gut-level feeling about the teacher's practice. In fact, the process of writing a CEIJ argument can help you clarify whether your concerns about a teacher are rooted in substantial evidence of poor performance, based on limited evidence that requires further substantiation, or rooted mainly in personal annoyances that should not trigger a negative evaluation. You might start by articulating your most blunt (even unprofessional) feelings about the teacher's practice, for example, "Mrs. Smith's classroom is a disaster. She has no control, the kids are awful to each other (even though they're great kids outside of her class), and they can never focus on learning. She wastes the whole lesson dealing with conflicts that should have been prevented in the first place."

Clearly, this type of statement can't appear in a formal evaluation—but if it reflects how you actually feel, it can be a useful starting point because it will allow you to examine your perceptions in light of the evidence you have on hand.

The next step is to convert each statement into professional language that you can validate with evidence. For example, "Mrs. Smith's classroom is a disaster" might become, "Mrs. Smith has failed to establish a classroom climate conducive to learning." The claim, "She wastes the whole lesson dealing with conflicts that should have been prevented in the first place" could be restated as, "Mrs. Smith does not deal effectively with student misconduct." And, "She has no control, the kids are awful to each other, and they can never focus on learning" could become, "As a result, students spend significant time off task and engaged in conflict." Each of these revised statements uses appropriate terminology, and you can demonstrate or refute them with evidence. If you find that you lack such evidence, you may want to conduct additional formal observations, and if you still don't have clear evidence to support the claim, you will need to revise your claim.

Finally, you may need to revise your claim a second time to use the specific language of your evaluation criteria. You may find that you naturally write using language from a variety of professional sources, but some of this language may not align with your actual evaluation criteria. For example, you may expect teachers to apply what they have learned in professional development, but if it's not in the evaluation criteria, it's unlikely to withstand scrutiny, and is therefore best to exclude from formal evaluations.

Repeat the CEIJ writing process for each area in which the teacher's practice is unsatisfactory. You may find that negative ratings on just one or two criteria are required to trigger an overall negative evaluation and begin the process for probation or nonrenewal. Check with your supervisor, legal counsel, and human resources department to establish clarity on the process in your school or district.

High-stakes evaluations do not and should not result in dismissal every time. The CEIJ format can be helpful for any high-stakes evaluation— not just those that are a step toward dismissal. If you can connect related areas of underperformance, you can craft both a stronger argument and articulate a clearer path to improvement. For example, if you discern that a teacher's poor planning is contributing to his struggles with classroom management, clarifying this with CEIJ will help the teacher understand how to improve. If the teacher has tried to improve his classroom management using only rewards and consequences, seeing the connection between lesson planning and student behavior could be transformative. This combination of accountability and support increases the probability that other decision makers, such as school board members, will support your decision.

In most cases, you'll want to resist the temptation to write an evaluation that is strongly negative in all areas. You should never issue such an evaluation unless the situation warrants it and you have adequate evidence for each criterion; otherwise, the evaluation will appear to be based on personal animosity rather than reality. Often, teachers who are underperforming in one area are perfectly satisfactory in other areas; for example, a teacher with poor classroom management skills may have excellent relationships with colleagues. If you attempt to give low marks in areas in which the teacher is actually proficient, you will undermine the credibility of the entire evaluation, making it more likely to be overturned if appealed.

To craft effective final evaluations, use the CEIJ format when appropriate, but don't overdo it. If a teacher is satisfactory in some areas, you can use the CEIJ format for consistency, or provide more general statements indicating your lack of concern in those areas. Again, you may only need to document one or two unsatisfactory areas in order to take the action you feel will most benefit students. And by all means, if you discover as a result of the CEIJ writing process that your concerns are too limited in scope to justify an overall negative evaluation, consider using a coaching approach rather than the evaluation process to help the teacher make the necessary improvements.

To learn more about Jon Saphier's CEIJ approach, see his 1993 book *How to Make Supervision and Evaluation Really Work: Supervision and Evaluation in the Context of Strengthening School Culture.*

Day 17 Action Challenge: Identify High-Stakes Teachers

Make a confidential list of the 20 percent of teachers whose evaluations you currently view as high stakes—teachers who are new, clearly struggling, or marginal. Keep this list to yourself, and use it to guide your evidence collection and formal evaluations. Don't treat these teachers differently, but take extra care in compiling all of the evidence you'll need if corrective action becomes necessary. As you continue your classroom visits and converse with teachers, keep your focus on the evidence from the visit, and strive to make clearer, more explicit references to your instructional framework.

You may want to consider the following questions for reflection.

- Which teachers do I know the least about? How much time have I spent in their classrooms so far?

- When have I been surprised by a performance issue late in the school year? What warning signs did I miss? What caused me to overlook these warning signs?

- What indicators give me confidence that a teacher can safely be considered low stakes?

Identifying Improvements From Classroom Visits

A s we've explored throughout this book, visiting classrooms—observing teaching, and talking with teachers—is one of the most impactful ways instructional leaders can spend their time. While the immediate focus of a classroom visit may be to help the individual teacher reflect and grow, and repeated visits throughout the year can lead to higher-quality final evaluations, the benefits aren't limited to our work with individual teachers. In this chapter, we'll explore the ways spending time in classrooms every day can help us build relational trust, make better decisions, and build a common vision. This will help instructional leaders identify necessary improvements, strengthen leadership, and increase teachers' impact on learning.

Build Relational Trust

School leaders everywhere learn to be visible around campus, but the high-performance instructional leadership model goes further by emphasizing substantive, frequent visits to classrooms, followed by evidence-based conversations with teachers. A key reason these conversations are so powerful—in addition to their direct impact on teacher growth—is their contribution to *relational trust*.

In their book *Trust in Schools: A Core Resource for Improvement*, Anthony Bryk and Barbara Schneider (2002) describe *relational trust* as "a particular system of social exchanges" that is distinct from the contractual trust that exists between, say, a business and its customers (p. 16). Relational trust grows as staff become better able to discern the intentions and predict the future behavior of their colleagues. This discernment is based on both beliefs about others and direct observation of their behavior. Bryk and Schneider (2002) explain how relational trust can be damaged:

> Relational trust diminishes when individuals perceive that others are not behaving in ways that can be understood as consistent with their expectations about the other's role obligations. Moreover, fulfillment of obligations entails not only "doing the right thing," but also doing it in a respectful way, and for what are perceived to be the right reasons. (p. 21)

Instructional leaders who don't regularly visit and converse with teachers have fewer opportunities to establish relational trust, and when teachers have limited information about leaders' actions and intentions, assumptions will fill in the gaps.

There is simply no substitute for engaging in purposeful, frequent conversations about teaching and learning. The more instructional leaders visit classrooms and talk with teachers, the stronger their professional relationships will be, and the higher the level of relational trust in the school will be. Bryk and Schneider (2002) identify four important benefits of this relational trust at the organizational level.

First, relational trust reduces the risk of change and serves as a catalyst for innovation. Second, relational trust makes it easier to make decisions and resolve conflicts; Bryk and Schneider (2002) note that this occurs "because of the assumed good intentions all around" (p. 33). Third, relational trust contributes to clear, shared expectations for behavior and a high degree of self-monitoring by staff, so less top-down effort is necessary for upholding expectations. Fourth, relational trust creates a moral imperative to go above and beyond contractual requirements to support the mission of the organization.

While it's difficult to overstate the value of relational trust for the overall functioning of the school, classroom visits and conversations between instructional leaders and teachers also provide detailed information about teaching and learning that can inform the large number of specific decisions that leaders make on a day-to-day basis.

Use Classroom Visits to Enable Better Decision Making

Instructional leaders who are in classrooms frequently have access to information that they would not otherwise have. As you develop the habit of visiting classrooms every day, you'll gain vastly more knowledge about each teacher's strengths and needs. This information enables one of your most essential roles as an instructional leader: your decision-making role (Mintzberg, 1973). While you can delegate many of the tasks you perform on a day-to-day basis to others or encode them in school policies and procedures, many decisions continue to require your attention because you have information that others in your school simply do not have.

This information comes from two sources: (1) communication built on trust, and (2) observation of classroom practices. First, regular visits increase trust, and trust strengthens the lines of communication that allow relevant information to flow to instructional leaders. In other words, stronger relationships naturally result in more communication because relationships increase everyone's confidence that investing time and effort in communication will be worthwhile. Second, classroom visits themselves provide firsthand information about what is taking place in classrooms. This informs decisions about students, staff, and all manner of professional development and operational decisions. Being in classrooms on a daily basis gives you a great deal more knowledge about each teacher's practice, as you have probably witnessed by now, so you can more effectively influence their growth and evaluation. It also allows you to identify trends that can inform professional development—especially if you intentionally visit each teacher during a certain subject or focus on a specific practice.

Instructional leaders who are in classrooms frequently have access to information that they would not otherwise have.

But these benefits aren't limited to instructional decision making; time in classrooms can even inform logistical decisions such as how to optimize the bell schedule. Most school administrators spend only a small proportion of their time on activities explicitly related to instructional leadership, with the balance devoted to all manner of operational matters (Grissom et al., 2013). They can make these operational decisions more effectively if they have ample and appropriate background knowledge stemming from regular visits to classrooms. Simply put, being in classrooms provides a level of insight that you can't obtain any other way.

Build a Common Vision

Ultimately, increased time in classrooms can lead to the development of a focused and shared vision for the school. When instructional leaders demonstrate that they're not only visible but also paying attention to what teachers and students need, they enlist a level of support that can be truly transformative. Too often, schools operate primarily on the basis of contractual trust, with everyone doing their jobs, but not necessarily working toward a closely shared vision (Bryk & Schneider, 2002).

When instructional leaders spend time in classrooms and talk with teachers daily, we have the opportunity to both learn from and influence the teachers we serve and support, and this, more than any other factor, catalyzes the formation of a coherent, deeply held, and broadly shared vision for the school.

Day 18 Action Challenge: Identify Your Biggest Insights From Classroom Visits

What are the most important insights you've gained from your visits to classrooms so far? Identify at least six insights based on your time in classrooms and your conversations with teachers.

You may want to consider the following questions for reflection.

- What aspects of our instructional framework am I now more familiar with as a result of my classroom visits and conversations with teachers?
- What operational decisions have I been able to make because of my time in classrooms?
- What are some implications for upcoming professional development, based on what I've learned from my visits?

19

Opening the Door to New Models of Professional Learning

Your practice of visiting classrooms daily and engaging in conversation about instruction is valuable for strengthening trust and improving decision quality. But it also opens the door to new possibilities for professional development that deprivatize practice and accelerate professional learning—and teachers who are accustomed to being left alone wouldn't welcome these practices. Too many classrooms operate as silos, with each teacher working independently, unaware of what his or her colleagues are doing or how they could improve their work together—or, as Robert Eaker puts it, "as a collection of independent contractors united by a common parking lot" (as cited in Schmoker, 2006, p. 23). The same is true of entire schools, and even districts. But when we set new norms of transparency and dialogue, we can explore new models of collaboration and professional development that take advantage of our most abundant and untapped resource for learning: each other. In this chapter, we'll review several techniques and models for making practice more transparent and ways to minimize the natural fear and defensiveness that may accompany early efforts. We will discuss celebrating exemplary teacher practice, sharing practice-focused video clips, facilitating instructional rounds, and engaging in student shadowing. These strategies build on the trust that you're establishing with your teachers, one conversation at a time, and encourage them to extend this type of trust to each other.

Celebrate Exemplary Practice in Meetings and in Writing

We often celebrate staff members' noninstructional contributions, like organizing events, but rarely celebrate achievement and contributions in the core work of teaching. When you visit classrooms daily, you'll have plenty to celebrate publicly. An early step in deprivatizing practice is to simply share the best of what you're seeing in classrooms using your existing platforms. When you start a faculty meeting or professional development session, take a moment to congratulate and honor teachers for specific, noteworthy accomplishments and practices that you've noticed during your classroom visits.

Celebration rituals are powerful culture-building activities. In my school, I would often begin faculty meetings by bringing gerbera daisies or stem roses—or in the fall, miniature pumpkins and gourds—and giving them out to honor specific faculty members. The exact type of token doesn't matter—in fact, it often elicited a chuckle when a teacher would receive a lumpy gourd, or when a male teacher received a rose. The message is what matters. When you devote time and effort to recognizing what teachers are doing, they take notice.

> *Celebration rituals are powerful culture-building activities.*

Publicly honoring teachers for instructional excellence can be tricky, because it has the potential to raise concerns of favoritism. Even the teacher being honored may resent being singled out. And when you're honoring improvement rather than excellence, teachers who perceive themselves to be stronger than the teacher you're honoring may feel slighted. To avoid these pitfalls with a traditional kudos, you may want to try the following approach, which focuses on celebrating your learning rather than the teacher directly.

In your public comments to staff about your class visits, which you'll make after your first complete cycle, you'll frame the purpose of your visits as learning, to make you a more effective leader (see chapter 4, page 35). This lays an excellent foundation for public celebration: rather than compliment teachers directly, you can highlight what you've *learned* from visiting their classes and having conversations with them. By moving the spotlight slightly off of the individual teacher and onto the teaching and learning dynamics you discussed, you indirectly honor the teacher, without creating awkwardness.

For example, rather than say "Mrs. Smith had a fantastic lesson on fractions the other day—great job using formative assessment, Mrs. Smith!" you could instead focus on what you learned from the experience: "I was visiting Mrs. Smith's class the other day during a lesson on fractions, and I was struck by the importance of formative assessment. In our follow-up conversation, we talked about what we do with formative assessment data, and I realized that a lot of the value of formative assessment comes from the insights it gives us about student misconceptions. So, I want to thank Mrs. Smith for modeling the use of formative assessment for me, and for having that conversation about how she uses formative assessment to address students' misconceptions effectively." You can then ask Mrs. Smith to come to the front of the room to receive a token of appreciation and a round of applause.

Note that this approach focuses the faculty's attention on what you learned, rather than on Mrs. Smith's teaching. Because you're not sharing many details about what Mrs. Smith said or did, you can use this structure regardless of what actually happened, which gives you tremendous flexibility. If Mrs. Smith was in fact resistant to thinking about formative assessment and student misconceptions, she'll get the message that it's an important topic—and she now has a reputation to live up to. If Mrs. Smith knows she's your school's leading expert on formative assessment, she'll feel that she has been acknowledged respectfully, without being put on a pedestal. If Mrs. Smith is making progress in her use of formative assessment, but isn't outstanding, you'll have acknowledged her efforts and progress. No matter what, everyone will get the message that he or she should be thinking about formative assessment, and should be prepared to engage fully in conversations with you.

You can also share these kudos in your regular newsletter. When I was a teacher, my principal devoted a full page of her newsletter each week to listing the various contributions staff members had made to the school community. If you write about the learning you're engaging in with specific teachers, you're not only deprivatizing practice, but also encouraging others to strive for excellence in the same areas.

Over the course of a cycle of visits, you may identify patterns that are worth commenting on in a dedicated *instructional letter*. For example, if you see certain practices for formative assessment working well in several classrooms, you may write a two- or three-page letter detailing what you saw and why it worked, and explicitly encourage other staff to strive to use the same practices. This is especially effective as a means of preparing teachers for upcoming professional development. Over time, focused instructional letters can lead to tighter schoolwide definitions of key instructional practices, as well as a greater sense among staff of your vision for teaching and learning.

Share Practice-Focused Video Clips

Most teachers meet regularly with their colleagues to talk about curriculum, assessments, and student progress, but rarely—if ever—do teachers actually see each other teaching. The simplest and least-threatening approach to giving teachers a firsthand view of each other's practice is using video to share carefully selected clips for feedback and discussion.

On a practical level, video eliminates the need for teachers to give up a planning period or arrange for substitute coverage in order to observe their colleagues. Video is easier than ever to capture and share, thanks to ubiquitous smartphones and software. A variety of specially designed applications and online services is available to make it easy to share video quickly and securely; please visit www.instructionalleadershipchallenge.com/video for current recommendations.

But an even greater advantage of video is the feeling of safety and control it creates for teachers who may be hesitant to seek peer feedback. When teachers seek feedback, they aren't asking for unsolicited suggestions and criticism; they want a trusted perspective on specific issues and aspects of their practice. During an in-person observation, all manner of issues may come to the observer's attention, and it's very difficult to limit comments and feedback to the teacher's specific areas of interest. With video, teachers seeking feedback can film only the relevant portion of the lesson and can even edit out portions they'd prefer not to share. Teachers can also decide not to share the video at all if the lesson doesn't go well; they can simply try again if they want to present a better example for feedback. This ability to selectively share professional practice, and even have a complete do-over, is considerably less threatening than inviting a peer to observe in person.

> *When teachers seek feedback, they aren't asking for unsolicited suggestions and criticism; they want a trusted perspective on specific issues and aspects of their practice.*

Even if sharing video is optional, instructional leaders play a crucial role in encouraging and facilitating this form of collaboration among teachers. Here are three steps you can take to ensure that teachers have the opportunity to benefit from video-based professional learning.

First, make sure they have access to appropriate technology (including Internet access and software). Many smartphones and video cameras record video in high definition, which may result in large files and long transfer times. Recording with an app such as Sibme, which is optimized to produce small files, can make it vastly simpler to share video. Please visit www.instructionalleadershipchallenge.com/video for current recommendations.

Second, make sure teachers choose a specific focus for their collaboration, rather than seeking general feedback. Open-ended invitations to provide feedback are likely to cause hurt feelings and increase teachers' reluctance to share in the future. Before sharing videos, teachers should select a specific practice that they'd like feedback on and formulate specific questions for their colleagues to answer.

Third, start with your most eager volunteers. As the first collaborators find success in their joint work, the word will spread—and the practice will spread, too. Resist the temptation to make this—or any of the other practices in this chapter—mandatory at the outset.

Facilitate Instructional Rounds

The practices of *instructional rounds* (City et al., 2009) and *teacher rounds* (Teitel, 2013; Troen & Boles, 2014) have emerged as an attempt to replicate the value of hospital rounds conducted by physicians. Typically, a group of educators will visit a number of classrooms across a school or district and then discuss what they observed. Rather than help teachers improve their individual practice, rounds models facilitate organizational learning at the school level, or among schools working together in improvement networks.

For leaders seeking to facilitate rounds among teachers and other staff within a school, two resources I recommend are *The Power of Teacher Rounds: A Guide for Facilitators, Principals, and Department Chairs* (Troen & Boles, 2014) and *School-Based Instructional Rounds: Improving Teaching and Learning Across Classrooms* (Teitel, 2013). For districts and other entities seeking to start cross-school and cross-district rounds, the authoritative guide is *Instructional Rounds in Education: A Network Approach to Improving Teaching and Learning* (City et al., 2009).

When facilitating rounds in your school or district, strive to keep the focus on the teaching and learning dynamics you're noticing. Observers will naturally tend to use judgmental language when discussing what they've seen, and this can lead to unproductive debates about teacher performance that aren't grounded in sufficient context or evidence. Instead, focus on using the language of your instructional framework—drawing on your teacher evaluation criteria, curricular expectation, and past professional development—to describe and analyze what you've seen, rather than to evaluate the teacher. For example, if your rounds group observes a lesson in which students are discussing the causes of the Civil War, you can refer to your instructional framework for language about question and discussions. Rather than try to evaluate the teacher's practice, use this language to discuss the evidence. For example, you might refer to Danielson's (2007) domain 3, component B, *using questioning and discussion techniques*: "I noticed that the teacher was challenging students to justify their thinking—for example, when she said . . ."

You may also find it helpful to choose a specific focus—such as rigor, engagement, or some other characteristic of good teaching—for your group. The advice in chapter 20 on choosing a focus for a cycle of classroom visits (page 175) applies equally well to instructional rounds groups.

Engage in Student Shadowing

Finally, a simple model for deprivatizing practice and identifying school-level areas for improvement is student shadowing. The goal of shadowing is to see schooling as students experience it by going from class to class throughout the day with a specific student (Ginsberg, 2011). Shadowing can be especially valuable for understanding the unique experiences of students who receive special education or English learner services, which may differ markedly from the experiences of other students (Soto, 2012). Any staff member can participate in shadowing, and you may want to have a group of staff shadow different students on the same day, then meet after school to compare notes. It's best to have no more than one adult shadowing an individual student, to avoid creating too great a disruption in the student's day.

Shadowing can reveal a great deal about a student's social and academic experiences, and for this reason, it's best to approach shadowing with a clear plan in mind and obtain the support of individual students in advance. For more specific guidance on student shadowing, see *Transformative Professional Learning: A System to Enhance Teacher and Student Motivation* (Ginsberg, 2011) and *ELL Shadowing as a Catalyst for Change* (Soto, 2012). You may want to shadow a student to gain a general sense of the student's daily experience, or you may want to choose a particular focus; follow the guidelines in chapter 20 to ensure that your focus is productive.

> *Shadowing can reveal a great deal about a student's social and academic experiences, and for this reason, it's best to approach shadowing with a clear plan in mind and obtain the support of individual students in advance.*

As with instructional rounds, the goal of shadowing students is not to evaluate individual teachers, but to facilitate organizational learning. Since teachers may have questions or concerns about the presence of visitors in their classrooms, see Ginsberg (2011) and Soto (2012) for additional guidance on planning and facilitating student shadowing.

Although there are many other models for professional learning and collaboration, the models I highlight in this chapter are especially powerful in deprivatizing practice, increasing professional learning, identifying patterns, and facilitating better decision making on behalf of students.

Day 19 Action Challenge: Share the Highlights

Draft an instructional letter or a brief article in your regular staff newsletter to highlight the best of what you've seen so far in your classroom visits. Or, if you have a scheduled staff meeting planned for today, briefly share your insights and next steps with your entire faculty. Keep the focus entirely positive, and emphasize how much you're learning from visiting classrooms and talking with teachers.

You may want to consider the following questions for reflection.

‣ What have I noticed from my visits that I'm most excited to share with staff?

‣ What activities from this chapter would best help teachers become more aware of each other's strengths?

‣ What activities from this chapter would help us identify areas in which to make improvements as a school?

Choosing an Instructional Focus for an Observation Cycle

After finishing your second cycle of classroom visits, you may want to continue using an open-ended approach in your third cycle and beyond, or you may want to choose a specific schoolwide instructional focus. Having a focus is optional; there's nothing wrong with continuing to engage each teacher on specific issues relevant to their practice, rather than trying to focus on one aspect of instruction with all teachers. But choosing a focus can provide powerful information for school improvement efforts and can create a sense of unity and momentum among your staff. If you do want to choose a focus for your next cycle of classroom visits, keep the following criteria in mind: broad relevance, observability, and strategic impact. This chapter will also discuss some cautions to keep in mind when using instructional strategies.

Ensure Broad Relevance

First, your focus must be relevant the majority of the time and in the majority of classes. If you intend to spend a significant amount of time checking for, documenting about, and communicating over a particular issue, it's essential to choose an issue you have a strong chance of observing in nearly every classroom visit. If you decide to focus on how teachers handle student misconceptions, for example, you may become frustrated when you discover that students don't exhibit misconceptions very often in some classes, such as art or physical education. This may be acceptable if you're willing to leave some teachers out of your schoolwide focus; however, you should choose a focus that's relevant to every class.

You may find it helpful to think in terms of conditions for learning or qualities that you can detect when you walk into the room. For this reason, classroom climate issues are often a good focus because they're relevant at all times in all grade levels and subject areas—we always want the climate to be positive. For example, if students are engaged in focused, purposeful work, you'll be able to tell right away, regardless of the subject or activity. If students are being respectful toward each other, you'll be able to tell, regardless of the activity.

On the other hand, some overly specific conditions aren't as appropriate for a focus because they simply aren't appropriate at all times, or may represent only one point on a spectrum of appropriate ways to teach under different circumstances. For example, I often caution leaders against judging the rigor of a lesson based on simplistic factors such as the level of questions teachers are asking students according to Bloom's taxonomy. On one occasion when I was working with a group of administrators, I saw that they were marking teachers down for asking lower-level questions and telling them that such questions were not rigorous enough. However, low-level questions can be appropriate for some purposes, such as review. As with any instructional strategy, a teacher should use a higher-order question when it achieves his or her instructional purposes, not because it's superior to all alternatives under all circumstances. If you choose a focus such as rigor, be sure to adopt an appropriately broad definition that respects the fact that teachers must address a wide variety of instructional situations.

Establish Observability

Next, think about what might serve as evidence of the quality or condition you're focusing on—or of its absence. Is it observable? Can you discern it from talking with students or listening to their conversations with classmates? For example, coherent unit planning may be important, but it will be difficult to gain a sense of a unit's trajectory if you only visit for a few minutes every few weeks. Many characteristics of good teaching practice are not directly observable during classroom visits because they occur behind the scenes.

Some instructional issues may be observable only with careful planning on your part. For example, if you decide to focus on whether teachers are communicating clear objectives for each lesson, but you often miss the beginning of the lesson, you may not be able to gather the information you need. If you choose a focus that is only relevant at certain times in a lesson, such as the beginning, you may need to revise your schedule to ensure that you always see that part of the lesson, and if teachers vary their schedules from day to day—as is often the case in elementary schools—you may need to communicate and coordinate with teachers to ensure that you arrive in time.

Confirm Strategic Impact

Finally, when choosing a focus, look for opportunities to gather information aligned with your school's strategic priorities for improvement. Teaching is a complex endeavor, with a near-infinite number of potential focal issues. Strive to identify a focus that will give you the information you need to make decisions and take action that will lead to significant, long-term improvements in your school. Avoid reducing your classroom visits to data-collection walkthroughs focused on overly specific instructional strategies.

Strive to identify a focus that will give you the information you need to make decisions and take action that will lead to significant, long-term improvements in your school.

For example, if you've identified student engagement as a key issue impacting your school's overall performance, don't adopt a narrow focus on a minor engagement technique that may not move the needle. Use your classroom visits to address student engagement in all its breadth and complexity— for example, look for evidence of the full range of ways teachers are promoting engagement, and strive to develop a richer understanding of how these approaches work. Focus on the big opportunities, so your visits to classrooms will have an impact on your school's strategic priorities.

A Word of Caution About Instructional Strategies

A word of caution against choosing a specific instructional strategy as your focus: if you observe for a specific instructional strategy, you'll likely encounter several barriers. If you make brief visits to classrooms, it's unlikely that you'll be able to see that strategy in use very often. This can be frustrating because we often want to reinforce the instructional strategies teachers have been learning in recent professional development sessions. But consider how long it takes to use a given strategy, such as a questioning technique. Even if all teachers have relevant class discussions in every period, the technique may only take a minute or two to use. If you're in the classroom for ten minutes out of a fifty-minute period, you stand only a 20 percent chance of seeing the technique in action.

To make matters more complicated, if you tell staff that you're visiting to see how they're using that technique, teachers will go to great lengths to show you what you want to see when you're in the classroom. They may use the strategy immediately when you visit, but the rest of the time, they'll know they're off the hook because they've already shown off for you. If you want to check if teachers are implementing what they learned in professional development with fidelity, simply ask them. Teachers can provide better information on strategy use than you could ever collect yourself.

Day 20 Action Challenge: Choose a Focus for Cycle Three

Decide whether to have a focus for your third cycle of classroom visits, and if so, select a focus appropriate for all grades and subject areas. If you choose not to adopt a particular focus, you may want to invite teachers to individually request feedback on a particular aspect of their practice. If you're using the notecard system I described in chapter 6 (page 59), write the requested feedback topic on that teacher's index card.

You may want to consider the following questions for reflection.

- ‣ What qualities or conditions do I want to see at all times in all classrooms?
- ‣ What might I see that could serve as evidence of this quality or condition?
- ‣ What area of focus would have the biggest impact on teaching and learning?

21

Scaling Classroom Visits Across Your School and District

L eaders go first. You may not be the only—or the most senior—instructional leader in your school, but by being the first to develop a daily habit of classroom visits, you'll play an important role in the transformation of your school's professional culture. After you've made it a habit, it's time to scale the practice across your school's leadership team and across your professional network—whether that's a district, a diocese, a charter network, a regional service provider, or a state association. This chapter will discuss ways to scale your method of classroom visits across your school and network.

Scale Within Your School

If you're the sole administrator in your school, you may be the only instructional leader who engages in daily classroom visits. But keep an open mind; you may find that other staff are eager to get into classrooms, too—or at least willing to give it a try. Since the high-performance instructional leadership model centers on conversation and learning rather than directive feedback, it can be useful to a wide range of staff. If you have a counselor, for example, he or she may find it valuable to visit classrooms to see how specific students are doing throughout the day, and this may lead to rewarding conversations with teachers about how best to support them.

If you're an instructional coach looking for more entry points into classrooms, especially when teachers are resistant or don't think they need you, you may find that the high-performance instructional leadership model strengthens relationships and leads to more in-depth coaching engagements. If your responsibilities are explicitly nonsupervisory, it may help to frame your visits as a form of professional development for yourself rather than an effort to help teachers.

If you're part of an administrative team, strive to get everyone on board with visiting classrooms daily. The first—and most critical—step is to demonstrate that it's possible, by developing a consistent habit yourself. You may have already shared your intentions with your colleagues, but it's your example that will truly inspire change in others.

If you're not the principal, share this book with your principal, show how your classroom visits fit within your full schedule, and most important, show how they're impacting your relationships with your teachers and your knowledge of their practice.

If you are the principal, use both your example and your positional authority to make it an expectation. In collaboration with other leaders, agree to help run interference for each other, to minimize disruptions and ensure that everyone on your team gets into classrooms every day. This may be especially helpful to your assistant principals who bear primary responsibility for discipline; a few minutes of coverage can make all the difference. You may also find that increasing your presence in classrooms results in a reduction in office referrals.

Avoid the temptation to overspecialize your administrative roles at the secondary level; even administrators with primarily student-focused responsibilities should make daily visits to the teachers they evaluate, for two reasons. First, one administrator simply can't be as effective if he or she works with two or three times the normal number of teachers; the ratio matters. Second, classroom visits provide powerful professional development and important context for teacher evaluations. Every administrator who evaluates teachers should get into classrooms every day. Each administrator should visit only the teachers they evaluate, rather than try to get

Classroom visits provide powerful professional development and important context for teacher evaluations.

around to every classroom. While it can be helpful to see a wide range of classrooms, attempting to visit too many teachers in each cycle will reduce the frequency and total number of visits for each teacher, which diminishes the potential to build stronger relationships.

If you share a common vocabulary for teaching and learning, every member of your administrative team can accelerate everyone else's growth. If you're using an electronic app to take classroom notes and write observation reports, consider sharing these documents among your team so everyone has a chance to benefit from and contribute to a common professional vocabulary, and so you can provide more consistent, higher-quality written feedback.

Scale Across Your Network

To promote high-performance instructional leadership across your district, network, diocese, or association, share this book and the results you're getting. Give examples of the insights you've gained from talking with teachers after spending time in their classrooms, and explain how you've made time in your busy schedule. Your colleagues may look for "unfair" advantages that have allowed you to develop the habit of getting into classrooms daily, but don't let that dissuade you—convince them that they, too, can visit their teachers on a daily basis.

If you supervise principals and want daily classroom visits to be an expectation, don't assume it's happening. When you visit schools, of course principals will take you to visit classrooms, but that's not the goal; the goal is a daily habit, even when you're not there. You might want to use an electronic app so you have records—without requiring forms or other extra paperwork—of how often administrators are visiting classrooms.

To promote high-performance instructional leadership across your district, network, diocese, or association, share this book and the results you're getting.

Ultimately, if you're training school leaders how to visit classrooms, setting the expectation, and monitoring their frequency of classroom visits, you'll know vastly more about their practice, and they'll know vastly more about their teachers. All of you will make better decisions and enjoy stronger relationships.

Day 21 Action Challenge: Scale Up Your Success

Contact a colleague in your school, district, or organization who would benefit from the high-performance instructional leadership model, and share the successes you've experienced so far. Seek accountability in sustaining your habit of visiting classrooms daily, and work to scale the practice of visiting classrooms and talking with teachers across your organization.

You may want to consider the following questions for reflection.

- Who will be inspired to get into classrooms if I share my success?
- Who will help me maintain my commitment to visit classrooms three times a day?
- Who can help this practice spread in our network or region? How can we work together to get more people on board?

Building Capacity for Instructional Leadership

As you maintain the habit of visiting three classrooms a day and engaging in professionally rewarding conversations with teachers, you'll continue to build your school's capacity for instructional leadership. You'll enjoy an enhanced ability to make and implement decisions of all kinds because you'll have vastly more information about what's currently taking place in your school.

You may find that teachers occasionally ask you to provide feedback, but as we've seen, feedback often isn't what teachers need most. By engaging in evidence-based conversations in the context of a shared instructional framework, teachers will gain a wealth of insights about how they can improve their practice. Over time, you may find that they ask you more for support and resources than advice, yet you'll also find your ability to give advice and feedback greatly enhanced.

Ultimately, high-performance instructional leadership is about learning. The more we engage in classroom conversations with teachers, the more effectively we'll be able to lead learning and improvement in our schools.

Now that you understand the complete model, you may want to review chapter 5 to prepare for your third cycle of visits, in which you'll start to take notes and engage teachers in evidence-based conversations, using the language of your instructional framework.

If you haven't started your classroom visits yet, or if you've taken a few steps but haven't formed a consistent habit yet, now is the perfect time to start in earnest. Review the Action Challenges at the end of each chapter, and keep this book on hand so you can quickly review the model or the Action Challenges at any time.

Thank you for being among the thousands of instructional leaders from fifty countries around the world who are engaging in this work.

References and Resources

Allen, D. (2015). *Getting things done: The art of stress-free productivity*. New York: Penguin.

Bambrick-Santoyo, P. (2012). *Leverage leadership: A practical guide to building exceptional schools*. San Francisco: Jossey-Bass.

Baumeister, R. F., & Tierney, J. (2011). *Willpower: Rediscovering the greatest human strength*. New York: Penguin.

Bensoussan, B. E., & Fleisher, C. S. (2013). *Analysis without paralysis: 12 tools to make better strategic decisions* (2nd ed.). Upper Saddle River, NJ: FT Press.

Bryk, A. S., & Schneider, B. (2002). *Trust in schools: A core resource for improvement*. New York: Sage Foundation.

City, E. A., Elmore, R. F., Fiarman, S. E., & Teitel, L. (2009). *Instructional rounds in education: A network approach to improving teaching and learning*. Cambridge, MA: Harvard Education Press.

Danielson, C. (2007). *Enhancing professional practice: A framework for teaching* (2nd ed.). Alexandria, VA: Association for Supervision and Curriculum Development.

Danielson, C. (2015). *Talk about teaching! Leading professional conversations* (2nd ed.). Thousand Oaks, CA: Corwin Press.

Downey, C. J., Steffy, B. E., English, F. W., Frase, L. E., & Poston, W. K. (2004). *The three-minute classroom walk-through: Changing school supervisory practice one teacher at a time*. Thousand Oaks, CA: Corwin Press.

Duhigg, C. (2012). *The power of habit: Why we do what we do in life and business*. New York: Random House.

Ginsberg, M. B. (2011). *Transformative professional learning: A system to enhance teacher and student motivation*. Thousand Oaks, CA: Corwin Press.

Ginsberg, M. B. (2012). Stepping into a student's shoes. *Educational Leadership, 69*(5).

Grissom, J. A., Loeb, S., & Master, B. (2013). Effective instructional time use for school leaders: Longitudinal evidence from observations of principals. *Educational Researcher, 42*(8), 433–444.

Kachur, D. S., Stout, J. A., & Edwards, C. L. (2010). *Classroom walkthroughs to improve teaching and learning*. Larchmont, NY: Eye on Education.

Knight, J. (2011). *Unmistakable impact: A partnership approach for dramatically improving instruction*. Thousand Oaks, CA: Corwin Press.

Kruse, K. (2015). *15 secrets successful people know about time management: The productivity habits of 7 billionaires, 13 Olympic athletes, 29 straight-A students, and 239 entrepreneurs*. Philadelphia: Kruse Group.

Langley, G. J., Moen, R. D., Nolan, K. M., Nolan, T. W., Norman, C. L., & Provost, L. P. (2009). *The improvement guide: A practical approach to enhancing organizational performance*. San Francisco: Jossey-Bass.

Liker, J. K. (2004). *The Toyota way: 14 management principles from the world's greatest manufacturer*. New York: McGraw-Hill.

Marshall, K. (2013). *Rethinking teacher supervision and evaluation: How to work smart, build collaboration, and close the achievement gap* (2nd ed.). San Francisco: Jossey-Bass.

Mintzberg, H. (1973). *The nature of managerial work*. New York: Harper & Row.

MetLife. (2013). *The MetLife Survey of the American teacher: Challenges for school leadership*. New York: Author.

National Center for Education Evaluation and Regional Assistance. (2014). *State requirements for teacher evaluation policies promoted by Race to the Top* (NCEE Report No. 2014-4016). Accessed at http://files.eric .ed.gov/fulltext/ED544794.pdf on June 26, 2017. Washington, DC: Institute of Education Sciences.

Parkinson, C. N. (1957). *Parkinson's law, and other studies in administration*. Boston: Houghton Mifflin.

Saphier, J. (1993). *How to make supervision and evaluation really work: Supervision and evaluation in the context of strengthening school culture.* Acton, MA: Research for Better Teaching.

Schmoker, M. (2006). *Results now: How we can achieve unprecedented improvements in teaching and learning.* Alexandria, VA: Association for Supervision and Curriculum Development.

Schwartz, B. (2004). *The paradox of choice: Why more is less.* New York: Ecco.

Soto, I. (2012). *ELL shadowing as a catalyst for change.* Thousand Oaks, CA: Corwin Press.

Stone, D., & Heen, S. (2014). *Thanks for the feedback: The science and art of receiving feedback well (even when it is off base, unfair, poorly delivered, and frankly, you're not in the mood).* New York: Viking.

Teitel, L. (2013). *School-based instructional rounds: Improving teaching and learning across classrooms.* Cambridge, MA: Harvard Education Press.

Troen, V., & Boles, K. C. (2014). *The power of teacher rounds: A guide for facilitators, principals, and department chairs.* Thousand Oaks, CA: Corwin Press.

Washington State Legislature. (n.d.). *RCW 28A.405.100.* Accessed at http://app.leg.wa.gov/rcw/default.aspx?cite=28A.405.100 on February 10, 2017.

Zaleznik, A. (2004, January). Managers and leaders: Are they different? *Harvard Business Review.* Accessed at https://hbr.org/2004/01/managers -and-leaders-are-they-different on February 10, 2017.

Index

Messaging Matters
William D. Parker
Written for leaders, this title is divided into three parts, helping readers maximize their role as chief communicators with students, teachers, and parents and community.
BKF785

HEART!
Timothy D. Kanold
Use this resource to reflect on your professional journey and discover how to foster productive, heart-centered classrooms and schools.
BKF749

From Leading to Succeeding
Douglas Reeves
Utilizing the elements of effective leadership—purpose, trust, focus, leverage, feedback, change, and sustainability—education leaders can overcome any challenge.
BKF649

A Leader's Guide to Excellence in Every Classroom
John R. Wink
Explore the Hierarchy of Instructional Excellence and schoolwide support systems to help education leaders guarantee ultimate teacher success.
BKF719

GL◉BAL **PD**

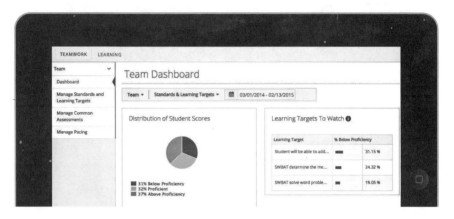

The **Power to Improve**
Is in Your Hands

Global PD gives educators focused and goals-oriented training from top experts. You can rely on this innovative online tool to improve instruction in every classroom.

- Get unlimited, on-demand access to guided video and book content from top Solution Tree authors.

- Improve practices with personalized virtual coaching from PLC-certified trainers.

- Customize learning based on skill level and time commitments.

▶ **REQUEST A FREE DEMO TODAY**
SolutionTree.com/GlobalPD

Solution Tree